LITURGY

PREPARATION

FOR 2005 (YEAR A)

BERNARD COTTER

LITURGY PREPARATION

FOR 2005 (YEAR A)

Resources for churches and schools

VERITAS

First published 2004 by
Veritas Publications
7/8 Lower Abbey Street
Dublin 1
Ireland
Email publications@veritas.ie
Website www.veritas.ie

ISBN 1 85390 845 2

A catalogue record for this book is available from the British Library.

Designed by Colette Dower
Printed in the Republic of Ireland by Betaprint, Dublin

Veritas books are printed on paper made from the wood pulp of managed forests. For every tree felled, at least one tree is planted, thereby renewing natural resources.

INTRODUCTION

I've always wanted a book like this.

As someone who has worked in parishes since I was ordained, I've always wanted a book I could open an hour or two before Mass time and find ideas to implement immediately. The ideal may be to prepare at the start of the week with the Parish Liturgy Group, but for all sorts of reasons this doesn't always happen. Instead, after a busy week of meetings, preparing couples for weddings, helping bereaved families, visiting the schools, as well as all the 'stuff' that just happens, I know that preparation for Sunday liturgies can easily be squeezed out. It's good to have a resource for a time like that.

I've seen many books like this, but none with a formula I could use: hence this different approach. The Opening Comments for the Mass are simple and straightforward, the introductions to the readings brief and to the point. The hymn suggestions are based on material that is either already known by, or available to, most choirs and congregations. I have tried to avoid liturgical ideas that would take a cast of thousands (and weeks of work) to turn into reality. Brevity and practicality were what I sought – and I hope both are provided in this publication. You can be the judge!

I developed most of the formulae used here in the pages of *Intercom*, where I wrote 'Presiders Pages' for sixty editions of the magazine. The late Fr Brian Magee CM helped me in the first few years, checking the pages before they went to print. His helpful advice shaped my approach to the Prayer of the Faithful. He allowed disagreement also: while he argued that prayers for the dead should always come last, my experience taught me that a long pause for silent prayer made a more effective conclusion to the intercessions. We agreed to differ on that — but I would still like to dedicate this book to his memory. May eternal peace be his.

I've always wanted a book like this. Now I have one. I hope to use it in many celebrations at Holy Family Church in Cork, during 2005, DV. I'll try to refine it for future use, and will welcome your suggestions and feedback (to frbernard@eircom.net) or to Veritas Publications.

Fr Bernard Cotter
Cork & Ross Diocese
Ireland

FIRST SUNDAY OF ADVENT

FOR PRESIDERS

Opening Comment

The season of Advent begins today. During the next twenty-seven days we will look forward in hope. We will watch for the end times, when Christ will come in glory, Christ whose birthday we will celebrate very soon.

Penitential Rite: Entering this time of waiting, let us remember God's faithfulness as we call to mind our sins...
Lord Jesus, you came to gather the nations into the peace of God's kingdom: Lord, have mercy.
You come in word and sacrament to strengthen us in holiness: Christ, have mercy.
You will come in glory with salvation for your people: Lord, have mercy.

Introduction to the Scripture Readings (Year A)

Isaiah 2:1-5 – Isaiah gives a prophecy of a time of peace when all people will worship the one God.
Romans 13:11-14 – Paul advises the Romans to live decent lives.
Matthew 24:37-44 – We're told to stay alert, because we don't know when the Master is coming.

The General Intercessions *(samples)*

Introduction *(by the Presider)*
Knowing that God is listening, let us make our prayers known.

Intercessions *(announced by the deacon, cantor or another person)*

1. For Christians everywhere, who await the Lord's return in glory,
    that they may be ready to meet him. *(Pause for silent prayer)*   Lord, hear us.

2. For the people in our world for whom there is no peace (especially N and N),
    that war may soon be a distant memory. *(Pause for silent prayer)*   Lord, hear us.

3. For those for whom this time of year brings anxiety, rather than happiness,
    that the peace of Christ may be theirs. *(Pause for silent prayer)*   Lord, hear us.

4. For people who are sick in mind or body,
    that the healing power of our God may touch them. *(Pause for silent prayer)*   Lord, hear us.

5. For all who have died (especially N & N),
    that eternal peace may be theirs. *(Pause for silent prayer)*   Lord, hear us.

Conclusion *(by the Presider)*
Loving God, you want what is best for your people:
Hear our prayers and help us in our needs, through Christ our Lord. Amen.

FOR LITURGY PLANNERS

Liturgical Suggestions

Bless the Advent wreath at the start of the first Mass of Advent in each church (see *The Veritas Book of Blessings*, page 21). At subsequent Masses, solemnly light one candle on the wreath at the start of Mass. The Jesse tree may also be blessed (see *The Veritas Book of Blessings*, page 117). Penitential Rite c-ii. No Gloria. First Opening Prayer. Year A readings. Preface of Advent 1. Eucharistic Prayer 3. Solemn Blessing 1 (Advent).

Songs: 'O Comfort My People'; 'O Come, O Come, Emmanuel'; 'Maranatha'.

The week ahead

Tuesday 30 November: St Andrew, Apostle (patron of fishermen).
Wednesday 1 December: World AIDS Awareness Day.
Thursday 2 December: International Day for the Abolition of Slavery.
Friday 3 December (First Friday): St Francis Xavier (patron of missionaries).

SECOND SUNDAY OF ADVENT

FOR PRESIDERS

Opening Comment

John the Baptist is the focus of the Gospel reading on the Second Sunday of Advent each year. His words challenge and inspire. We worship God who uses many messengers to call us from darkness to light.

Penitential Rite: As we prepare to listen to John the Baptist's message of repentance, let us call to mind our own need to repent... I confess...

Introduction to the Scripture Readings (Year A)

Isaiah 11:1-10 – Isaiah looks forward to the coming of a messiah, who will restore harmony and justice.
Romans 15:4-9 – Paul reminds us that the scriptures were written to teach about God's promises.
Matthew 3:1-12 – John the Baptist's call to repentance is described by Matthew.

The General Intercessions *(samples)*

Introduction *(by the Presider)*
Let us bring our prayers before God, who has pity on the weak.

Intercessions *(announced by the deacon, cantor or another person)*

1. For a spirit of repentance among all believers, we pray...
   (Pause for silent prayer)   Lord, hear us.

2. For peace where it is most lacking (especially in N.), we pray...
   (Pause for silent prayer)   Lord, hear us.

3. For reconciliation between those who are at war, we pray...
   (Pause for silent prayer)   Lord, hear us.

4. For our children, in this season of anticipation, we pray...
   (Pause for silent prayer)   Lord, hear us.

5. For all who are in need, we pray... *(Pause for silent prayer)*   Lord, hear us.

6. For those we have lost to death (especially N & N), we pray...
   (Pause for silent prayer)   Lord, hear us.

Conclusion *(by the Presider)*
O God, you save the poor when they cry to you:
Hear the prayers of all your people, through Christ our Lord. Amen.

FOR LITURGY PLANNERS

Liturgical Suggestions

The second purple candle of the Advent wreath is lit at the start of Mass. Penitential Rite a (Confiteor). Omit the Gloria. Alternative Opening Prayer. Preface of Advent 1 and Eucharistic Prayer 1. Or Eucharistic Prayer for Reconciliation 2 with its own preface. Solemn Blessing 1 (Advent).

Songs: 'O Come O Come Emmanuel'; 'The Lord Hears the Cry of the Poor'; 'The Lord Will Heal the Broken Heart'.

The Week ahead

Monday 6 December: St Nicholas (patron of children).
Tuesday 7 December: St Ambrose is honoured in Milan today.
Wednesday 8 December: Immaculate Conception (Holyday of Obligation). The eight-day Jewish feast of Hanukkah ('Festival of Lights') begins today.
Friday 10 December: International Human Rights Day (UN). Also Nobel Prize Day.

IMMACULATE CONCEPTION OF THE BVM

FOR PRESIDERS

Opening Comment

The feast of the Immaculate Conception recalls the conception of Mary, the mother of Jesus. We believe she was free from sin from the first moment of her life. We worship God, who delivers all people from the power of sin.

> *Penitential Rite: Let us remember God's great mercy as we call to mind our own need for forgiveness: (pause)*
> Lord Jesus, you are mighty God and Prince of Peace: Lord, have mercy.
> Lord Jesus, you are Son of God and Son of Mary: Christ, have mercy.
> Lord Jesus, you are Word made flesh and splendour of the Father: Lord, have mercy

Introduction to the Scripture Readings

Genesis 3:9-15, 20 – The story of Adam and Eve is read as a reminder of the origins of sin – and because Mary is often called 'the new Eve'.
Ephesians 1:3-6, 11-12 – Paul describes God's marvellous plan of salvation, in which Mary had a crucial role.
Luke 1:26-38 – At the Annunciation Mary showed her openness to God's will.

The General Intercessions *(Samples)*

> **Introduction** *(by the Presider)*
> Let us bring our prayers to the Lord who works wonders.
>
> **Intercessions** *(announced by the deacon, cantor or another person)*
> 1. For the Church,
>   that its members may not be overcome by temptation. *(Pause for silent prayer)* Lord, hear us.
>
> 2. For the world,
>   that the reign of sin in the structures of society may be defeated.
>   *(Pause for silent prayer)*   Lord, hear us.
>
> 3. For mothers and their children, born and unborn,
>   that they may be preserved from every danger. *(Pause for silent prayer)*   Lord, hear us.
>
> 4. For those in need of special healing,
>   that the prayers of the Virgin may support them every day.
>   *(Pause for silent prayer)*   Lord, hear us.
>
> 5. For our brothers and sisters who have gone before us in faith (especially N & N),
>   that they may find a home in heaven, with Our Lady and the saints.
>   *(Pause for silent prayer)*   Lord, hear us.
>
> 6. A moment's quiet prayer for our own needs... *(Long pause for silent prayer)*   Lord, hear us.
>
> **Conclusion** *(by the Presider)*
> O Lord our God, you always remember your people,
> Hear the prayers we make in confidence, through Christ our Lord. Amen.

FOR LITURGY PLANNERS

Liturgical Suggestions

Two candles burn on the Advent wreath from before the start of Mass today. Advent decorations remain in place, but an icon or image of Mary may be decorated with flowers and lights. Penitential Rite c-iii. The Gloria is prayed. Preface of the Immaculate Conception. Eucharistic Prayer 2. Solemn Blessing 15 (The Blessed Virgin Mary).

Songs: 'When Creation Was Begun'; 'Sing A New Song Unto the Lord'; 'Magnificat'.

COMMUNAL PENANCE SERVICE FOR ADVENT 2004

Preparations

All priests taking part vest in alb and purple stole beforehand. Candles are lit: the church lights may be dimmed. Servers lead the entrance procession during the entrance song.

INTRODUCTORY RITES

Entrance Song (e.g. 'O come, O come, Emmanuel')

Greeting (e.g. The Lord be with you...)

Opening Comment *(by the Presider)*
'Welcome to this celebration of God's mercy, and of our reconciliation with God and one another.
Our service has four parts. After this brief introduction, we will listen to God's word and reflect on it. Then we will celebrate the Rite of Reconciliation, during which everyone will have the opportunity of going to Confession. The service will end with an Act of Thanksgiving.
Let us pray...'

Opening Prayer
(from the Rite of Penance*, choose from pages 115-117) Example:
Lord,
hear the prayers of those who call on you,
forgive the sins of those who confess to you
and in your merciful love
give us your pardon and your peace.
We ask this through Christ our Lord.
Amen.

LITURGY OF THE WORD

A selection of readings is given in the Rite of Penance*, pages 119 to 202. One reading may be sufficient — the call to repentance of St John the Baptist, from the Second or Third Sunday of Advent (Year A)

The **homily** *follows. See homily resources for the Second or Third Sunday of Advent in any publication.*

The **examination of conscience** *may take the form of a period of silence following the homily.*

Or the following may be used:
We are taught to love God and love each other:
1. Reflecting on my love of God:
    Is God important to me?
    Do I pray each day?
    Do I attend Mass when I should?

2. Reflecting on my love of others:
    Have I a genuine love for those around me?
    What kind of person am I to live with?
    Am I an honest worker?
    Do I use my time and talents well?

Let us pause a moment and call to mind our own sins...
(A long pause for silent reflection follows)

COMMUNAL PENANCE SERVICE
FOR ADVENT 2004

RITE OF RECONCILIATION

Confession of Sins
Let us confess our sinfulness to God and one another:
I confess…

A litany of repentance may be prayed (e.g. Rite of Penance* p. 232) or a song may be sung: e.g. 'God of Mercy and Compassion' *or a version of the* Kyrie (e.g. 'You were sent to heal the contrite, Lord, have mercy…' etc.)

The **Lord's Prayer** follows.

Individual Confessions
(As the priests take up their positions, standing in various locations around the church, the presider explains the procedure.)
You are now invited to make your Confession to the priest of your choice. Begin by saying to him:
'I am sorry for all my sins, especially for…'
Tell him your sins, listen to his advice and the penance he gives you, and hear him absolve your sins. Then return to your seat and pray for those still waiting to confess. When everyone has been absolved, we will pray together in thanksgiving.

The presider may add:
I invite you to pray the Act of Sorrow:
 'O my God, I am sorry for all my sins,
 For not loving others and not loving you.
 Help me to live like Jesus and not sin again.
 Amen.'

THANKSGIVING

(After the Confessions have been completed)

Psalm of Praise
*A responsorial psalm of praise is prayed, e.g. Psalm 125 from the Second Sunday of Advent, Year A. The **Magnificat** may be prayed responsorially, or sung. Or another hymn of thanksgiving may be used (e.g.* 'Now Thank We All Our God' *or* 'How Great Thou Art'.) *At the end of the Act of Thanksgiving, the church lights are turned on in full.*

A **Sign of Peace** is then exchanged.

The **Final Blessing** is given.

Dismissal
Go in peace to love and serve the Lord.
Thanks be to God.

Final Song: Instrumental music fills the church as priests and people leave.

**Rite of Penance/Gnás na hAithrí* was published by Veritas Publications in 1976.

THIRD SUNDAY OF ADVENT

FOR PRESIDERS

Opening Comment

Traditionally, this Sunday is called Gaudete Sunday, which means 'a day for rejoicing'. Advent is more than half over, and the day of the Lord's coming is nearer. We worship God who promises us joy without end.
   Penitential Rite: Confident of the happiness that lies in the future, let us remember our sins and repent...
   Lord Jesus, you came to gather the nations into the peace of God's kingdom: Lord, have mercy.
   You come in word and sacrament to strengthen us in holiness: Christ, have mercy.
   You will come in glory with salvation for your people: Lord, have mercy.

Introduction to the Scripture Readings

Isaiah 35:1-6, 10 – Isaiah looks forward to the Day of Joy, when God's power will be seen on earth.
James 5:7-10 – James reminds us to be patient, for the Lord's coming in glory will be soon.
Matthew 11:2-11 – Today's Gospel tells us that what Isaiah prophesied came to pass in the life of Jesus.

The General Intercessions *(samples)*

Introduction *(by the Presider)*
Let us bring our prayers to God, who raises up those who are bowed down.

Intercessions *(announced by the deacon, cantor or another person)*

1. For all Christians,
    that they may experience joy as they prepare for the Lord's coming.
    (Pause for silent prayer)   Lord, hear us.

2. For the blind, the lame, the diseased and the deaf,
    that the Lord may bring them healing and strength. *(Pause for silent prayer)*   Lord, hear us.

3. For children who are in need this day,
    that the generosity of the wealthy may lift them up. *(Pause for silent prayer)*   Lord, hear us.

4. For people who live in fear,
    that courage may be God's gift to them. *(Pause for silent prayer)*   Lord, hear us.

5. For those who have died (especially N & N),
    that they may be raised up to glory, we pray. *(Pause for silent prayer)*   Lord, hear us.

6. For our own needs, for those who have asked our prayers...
    (Long pause for silent prayer)   Lord, hear us.

Conclusion *(by the Presider)*
O God, you keep faith with those in need of your kindness and justice:
Receive the prayers we make, through Christ our Lord. Amen.

FOR LITURGY PLANNERS

Liturgical Suggestions

Today is Gaudete Sunday. Rose vestments may be worn, or the altar area may be decorated with a rose-coloured cloth or flowers. The lighting of the pink candle on the Advent wreath takes place at the start of Masses today. Penitential Rite c-ii. Omit Gloria. Alternative Opening Prayer. Preface of Advent 2. Eucharistic Prayer 3. Solemn Blessing 1 (Advent).

Songs: 'O Come, O Come, Emmanuel'; 'Wait for the Lord' (Taizé).

The Week ahead

Monday 13 December: St Lucy is honoured: her name means 'light'. People with eye ailments pray to St Lucy.
Tuesday 14 December: St John of the Cross, renowned spiritual writer and Doctor of the Church is honoured today.
Thursday 16 December: Mexican families remember Mary and Joseph's journey to Bethlehem by gathering for *Las Posadas*.

FOURTH SUNDAY OF ADVENT

FOR PRESIDERS

Opening Comment

The Season of Advent ends next Friday, so the celebration of the birth of Christ is now very close. We gather in preparation for that great event, worshipping God who was made flesh to bring us to glory.

Penitential Rite: As we prepare ourselves to celebrate God's immense love for us,
let us reflect on how ready we are to celebrate this great feast...

Lord Jesus, you came to gather the nations into the peace of God's kingdom: Lord, have mercy.
You come in word and sacrament to strengthen us in holiness: Christ, have mercy.
You will come in glory with salvation for your people: Lord, have mercy.

Introduction to the Scripture Readings

Isaiah 7:10-16 – Contains Isaiah's prophecy of the events we celebrate at Christmas – words repeated in today's Gospel.
Romans 1:1-7 – Paul begins his letter to the Romans by summing up the message of Advent and Christmas.
Matthew 1:18-24 – Matthew recalls some events that happened before the birth of Jesus.

The General Intercessions *(samples)*

Introduction *(by the Presider)*
Let us bring our prayers to the Lord, the King of Glory.

Intercessions *(announced by the deacon, cantor or another person)*

1. For all who follow Christ,
   that they may make their hearts ready for Christmas. *(Pause for silent prayer)*   Lord, hear us.

2. For parents who look forward to the birth of their offspring, as Joseph and Mary did,
   that they may have a safe delivery and the gift of a healthy child.
   (Pause for silent prayer)   Lord, hear us.

3. For our relatives and friends travelling home,
   that they may travel safely, and find rest and refreshment here.
   (Pause for silent prayer)   Lord, hear us.

4. For people who dread Christmas because of bereavement or loneliness,
   that our support may help them cope. *(Pause for silent prayer)*   Lord, hear us.

5. For those who have gone before us in faith (especially N & N),
   that they may share in Christ's resurrection from the dead.
   (Pause for silent prayer)   Lord, hear us.

6. For our own needs, for those who have asked our prayers...
   (Long pause for silent prayer)   Lord, hear us.

Conclusion *(by the Presider)*
O God, yours is the earth and its fullness:
Bless your people by hearing the prayers we make, through Christ our Lord. Amen.

FOR LITURGY PLANNERS

Liturgical Suggestions

The lighting of the fourth candle on the Advent wreath takes place at the start of Masses today. Penitential Rite c-ii. No Gloria. First Opening Prayer. Preface of Advent 2. Eucharistic Prayer 2. Solemn Blessing 1 (Advent).

Songs: 'O Come, O Come, Emmanuel'; 'Magnificat'; 'Maranatha'.

The Week ahead

Tuesday 21 December: Winter solstice: the shortest day of the year.
Thursday 23 December: The Emperor's Birthday is celebrated in Japan.

VIGIL MASS OF CHRISTMAS

FOR PRESIDERS

Opening Comment

We gather this evening in anticipation. The sun has set on this year's Advent and the night of Christmas has begun. Before this night has passed we will have joyfully celebrated the birth of the Light of the World, Jesus Christ, whose life, death and resurrection brought us salvation.

Penitential Rite: As we prepare to reflect on the mystery of God's wonderful love,
let us call to mind our need of divine grace to lift us up to glory: (pause)
Lord Jesus, you are mighty God and Prince of Peace: Lord, have mercy.
Lord Jesus, you are Son of God and Son of Mary: Christ, have mercy.
Lord Jesus, you are Word made flesh and splendour of the Father: Lord, have mercy.

Introduction to the Scripture Readings

Isaiah 62:1-5 – Isaiah writes of God marrying his people.
The best revelation of what this might mean is seen in Jesus, fully human, yet fully divine.
Acts 13:16-17, 22-25 – Paul shows how the birth of Jesus was part of God's plan – just as John the Baptist foretold.
Matthew 1:1-25 (full form) – The family tree of Jesus was a mix of saints and sinners – a family just like our own.
Matthew 1:18-25 (shorter form) – Joseph did what God asked him and Jesus was born to Mary – all according to God's plan.

The General Intercessions *(Samples)*

Introduction *(by the Presider)*
Sisters and brothers, as part of the family of God, we can ask for help in all our needs:

Intercessions *(announced by the deacon, cantor or another person)*

1. For those who will mark the birth of Christ all over the world this night,
    that the celebration may bring a new light to their lives. *(Pause for silent prayer)*   Lord, hear us.

2. For the people who live in lands scarred by war and violence,
    that the Son born this night may turn them away from aggression — to peace and love.
    (Pause for silent prayer)   Lord, hear us.

3. For the hungry, the sick and the homeless,
    that help, healing and friendship may be theirs. *(Pause for silent prayer)*   Lord, hear us.

4. For our community and our families,
    that those we love may share our faith in God,
    who took human form to show how we are cherished. *(Pause for silent prayer)* Lord, hear us.

5. For our friends who have fallen asleep in Christ (especially N & N),
    and for all we have known who have died since last Christmas, whom we remember now:
    (Pause for silent prayer)… that the peace and light of heaven may be theirs.   Lord, hear us.

6. For our own needs and for each other, we pray in silence…
    (Long pause for silent prayer)   Lord, hear us.

Conclusion *(by the Presider)*
God of light, we call you Emmanuel, God-with-us, and trust in your ever-loving care:
Hear our prayers and fill us anew with your light, we pray, through Christ our Lord, Amen.

FOR LITURGY PLANNERS

Liturgical Suggestions

The Advent wreath is removed on Christmas Eve. The crib is unveiled and blessed with holy water at the start of the Vigil Mass. See *The Veritas Book of Blessing Prayers*, page 56 or 57. Penitential Rite c-iii. Gloria. Preface of Christmas 1. Eucharistic Prayer 1 (with special form of *In union with the whole Church: we celebrate that **night**…*). Solemn Blessing 2 (Christmas).

Songs: Christmas Carols.

MIDNIGHT MASS

FOR PRESIDERS

Opening Comment

In the dark of this winter night, we proclaim the new light that has shone on the world: Jesus Christ is born! With the angels, we worship God who saves us — for through the life, death and resurrection of this child Jesus, salvation is ours.

Penitential Rite: As we enter into the mystery of God's wonderful love,
let us pause and call to mind our unworthiness in the light of this great night: (pause)
Lord Jesus, you are mighty God and Prince of Peace: Lord, have mercy.
Lord Jesus, you are Son of God and Son of Mary: Christ, have mercy.
Lord Jesus, you are Word made flesh and splendour of the Father: Lord, have mercy.

Introduction to the Scripture Readings

Isaiah 9:1-7 – The ancient promise of a light in darkness, a child born for us, is fulfilled this Christmas night.
Titus 2:11-14 – As we wait in hope for the Lord's coming in glory, we should live good and religious lives.
Luke 2:1-14 – As Jesus is born in Bethlehem, the shepherds recognise him and the angels echo their joy.

The General Intercessions (Samples)

Introduction (by the Presider)
Sisters and brothers, standing together in the brightness of this Christmas celebration,
let us ask God to fill the whole world with light.

Intercessions (announced by the deacon, cantor or another person)

1. For those who mark the birth of Christ all over the world this night,
    that the celebration may bring a new light to their lives. (*Pause for silent prayer*) Lord, hear us.

2. For all whose lives are darkened by war and violence (especially the people of N. and N.)
    that the peace and goodwill proclaimed by the angels
    may take root in their midst. (*Pause for silent prayer*)   Lord, hear us.

3. For the hungry, the sick and the homeless,
    and all whose loneliness seems more sharp at Christmas time,
    that the light Christ brought may brighten their lives. (*Pause for silent prayer*) Lord, hear us.

4. For our community and families,
    that Christ may find the same warm welcome among us
    as he received from Mary and Joseph and the shepherds that first Christmas night.
    (*Pause for silent prayer*)   Lord, hear us.

5. For our friends who have fallen asleep in Christ (especially N & N),
    and for all from this community who have died since last Christmas, whom we remember now:
    (*Pause for silent prayer*) that the peace and joy of heaven may be theirs.   Lord, hear us.

6. For our own needs and for each other, we pray...
    (*Long pause for silent prayer*)   Lord, hear us.

Conclusion (by the Presider)
Maker of heaven and earth, your Son is born for us, God from God, Light from Light, true God from true God: Hear the prayers we make with confidence, through the same Christ, our Lord, Amen.

FOR LITURGY PLANNERS

Liturgical Suggestions

If the Vigil Mass has not been celebrated, the crib is unveiled and blessed at the start of Midnight Mass: see *The Veritas Book of Blessing Prayers*, page 56 or 57. Incense is used. Penitential Rite c-iii. Gloria. Eucharistic Prayer 1 (with special form of *In union with the whole Church: we celebrate that **night**...*) Solemn Blessing 2 (Christmas).

Songs: Christmas Carols; 'Praise the Lord all You Nations'.

DAWN MASS

FOR PRESIDERS

Opening Comment

We gather with joy in our hearts to celebrate the birthday of our Saviour. The rising sun of this winter morning reminds us that Jesus who is born for us rose from death as our undying light, our hope and our salvation.

Penitential Rite: As we begin to celebrate the mystery of God's endless love,
let us remember our sinfulness in the light of divine grace...

Lord Jesus, you are mighty God and Prince of Peace: Lord, have mercy.
Lord Jesus, you are Son of God and Son of Mary: Christ, have mercy.
Lord Jesus, you are Word made flesh and splendour of the Father: Lord, have mercy.

Introduction to the Scripture Readings

Isaiah 62:11-12 – Isaiah proclaims the joy that comes with the Saviour's birth: God's people are to be redeemed, not forsaken.

Titus 3:4-7 – Paul reminds us that everything that has happened shows the compassion of God.

Luke 2:15-20 – Luke records that Jesus was first recognised by lowly shepherds – a sign of his future mission to people on the margins.

The General Intercessions *(Samples)*

Introduction *(by the Presider)*

As we acclaim the light that shines forth this day, let us bring our prayers to God.

Intercessions *(announced by the deacon, cantor or another person)*

1. For all who celebrate the birth of Christ this morning,
   that our commitment to Christ may grow each day. *(Pause for silent prayer)*   Lord, hear us.

2. For the people on the margins of our society,
   that, like the shepherds, they may lead us to Christ. *(Pause for silent prayer)*   Lord, hear us.

3. For pregnant women,
   that, like Mary, they may treasure the gift given in the birth of their child.
   (Pause for silent prayer)   Lord, hear us.

4. For newly-born babies and all our children,
   that they may know the friendship of Jesus throughout their lives.
   (Pause for silent prayer)   Lord, hear us.

5. For babies who have died and for all our dead (especially N & N),
   and for those we have known who have died since last Christmas, whom we remember now:
   (Pause for silent prayer)... that they may rise with Christ to glory.   Lord, hear us.

6. For our own needs and for each other, we pray ...
   (Long pause for silent prayer)   Lord, hear us.

Conclusion *(by the Presider)*

O God, we rejoice in you, we give glory to your holy name:
Hear our prayers and grant us your grace, through Jesus Christ our Lord. Amen.

FOR LITURGY PLANNERS

Liturgical Suggestions

Penitential Rite c-iii. Gloria. Preface of Christmas 1. Eucharistic Prayer 3. Solemn Blessing 2 (Christmas).

Songs: Christmas Carols; 'All the Ends of the Earth'.

CHRISTMAS DAY MASS

FOR PRESIDERS

Opening Comment

We celebrate today an amazing mystery — God is born in time. The eternal God has taken human flesh, has pitched his tent in the midst of humanity. With joy in our hearts, we contemplate the mystery of the Word made flesh.

Penitential Rite: As we prepare ourselves to ponder the mystery of God's wonderful love,
let us call to mind our sins: (pause)
Lord Jesus, you are mighty God and Prince of Peace: Lord, have mercy.
Lord Jesus, you are Son of God and Son of Mary: Christ, have mercy.
Lord Jesus, you are Word made flesh and splendour of the Father: Lord, have mercy

Introduction to the Scripture Readings

Isaiah 52:7-10 – Let there be great joy, because we have received Good News: God is consoling his people.
Hebrews 1:1-6 – Greater than all the angels is the firstborn Son of God, born in time today.
John 1:1-18 – In beautiful language, John describes the mystery of God taking on human flesh in Jesus.

The General Intercessions *(Samples)*

Introduction *(by the Presider)*
Let us bring our prayers to God, who has shown his salvation to the nations in the birth of Jesus.

Intercessions *(announced by the deacon, cantor or another person)*

1. For Christians all over the world, who gather to celebrate the Christmas feast,
   that they may follow Christ with enthusiasm through the year.
   (Pause for silent prayer)   Lord, hear us.

2. For the people for whom Christmas has little meaning,
   that they may accept the Good News of the Word made flesh.
   (Pause for silent prayer)   Lord, hear us.

3. For those with whom we will spend time this Christmas,
   that God may bless our families and all those we love. *(Pause for silent prayer)*   Lord, hear us.

4. For ourselves, as we hear the call to be messengers of the Gospel,
   that each day we may spread happiness and bring good news.
   (Pause for silent prayer)   Lord, hear us.

5. For those afflicted by illness or anxiety this Christmas,
   that the care of those around them may help them see God's compassion.
   (Pause for silent prayer)   Lord, hear us.

6. For our friends who have died (especially N & N),
   and for those we have known who have died since last Christmas, whom we remember now:
   (Pause for silent prayer) that the peace and light of heaven may be theirs.   Lord, hear us.

Conclusion *(by the Presider)*
O God, your love for your people is sure:
Hear our prayers and grant us your grace, through Christ our Lord. Amen.

FOR LITURGY PLANNERS

Liturgical Suggestions

Use incense at the principal Christmas Masses, honouring the altar, cross, crib, Gospel and gifts. Penitential Rite c-iii. Gloria. Preface of Christmas 1. Eucharistic Prayer 1 (with special form of *In union with the whole Church, we celebrate that* **day**...). Solemn Blessing 2 (Christmas).

Songs: Christmas Carols; 'How Lovely on the Mountains'; 'Sing a new Song unto the Lord'.

THE HOLY FAMILY OF JESUS, MARY AND JOSEPH

FOR PRESIDERS

Opening Comment
The day after Christmas Day is usually St Stephen's Day. But the Holy Family is the focus on the first Sunday after Christmas, so that celebration is kept today instead of the feast of Stephen. We worship God who shared the life of the human family, and thank God for all the gifts we continue to receive in each other.

> *Penitential Rite: Let us be thankful for the love in our families – and recall our own failure to show love: (pause)* I confess...

Introduction to the Scripture Readings
Ecclesiasticus 3:2-6, 12-14 – Those who look after their elderly or frail parents will be rewarded.
Colossians 3:12-21 – Family life works when people live in harmony. *(Last paragraph may be omitted – verses 18-21.)*
Matthew 2:13-15, 19-23 – Describes the early family life of Jesus, from his exile in Egypt to his childhood in Nazareth.

The General Intercessions *(Samples)*

Introduction *(by the Presider)*
Let us bring our prayers to God, who showers blessings upon all his sons and daughters.

Intercessions *(announced by the deacon, cantor or another person)*

1. For the members of the Christian family,
    that joy and peace may be theirs throughout the Christmas celebration.
    (Pause for silent prayer)   Lord, hear us.

2. For the families of this community,
    that members may learn to give way to each other in tolerance and respect.
    (Pause for silent prayer)   Lord, hear us.

3. For families where there is hurt and difficulty,
    that those who have suffered may find healing. *(Pause for silent prayer)*   Lord, hear us.

4. For families which live with illness and frailty,
    that those who are carers may be filled with gentleness and patience.
    (Pause for silent prayer)   Lord, hear us.

5. For the members of our families who have died (especially N & N),
    and for all those we knew who died during 2004, whom we remember now:
    (Pause for silent prayer) that the light of heaven may be theirs.   Lord, hear us.

6. For our own needs and for those in our prayers during the New Year celebrations ...
    (Long pause for silent prayer)   Lord, hear us.

Conclusion *(by the Presider)*
O God, your care for your family is constant:
Hear the prayers we make, in faith and trust, through Christ our Lord. Amen.

FOR LITURGY PLANNERS

Liturgical Suggestions
Penitential Rite a. Alternative Opening Prayer. The shorter form of the Second Reading is strongly recommended (omitting the last paragraph, verses 18-21). Preface of Christmas 2. Eucharistic Prayer 2. Solemn Blessing 3 (Beginning of the New Year).

Songs: Christmas Carols; 'My Soul Is Longing For Your Peace'; 'Lord of All Hopefulness'.

The Week Ahead
Tuesday 28 December: The Holy Innocents.
Saturday 1 January, 2005: New's Year's Day is World Day of Peace.

NEW YEAR'S DAY
SOLEMNITY OF MARY, MOTHER OF GOD

FOR PRESIDERS

Opening Comment

Happy New Year! On this first day of the Year of Our Lord 2005, we acclaim Mary as Mother of God and ask her to mind us and those we love during this new year. Today is also World Peace Day, a day during which we pray for peace.

Penitential Rite: As we prepare to celebrate this new start, let us acknowledge our sinfulness – and praise God's unending mercy: (pause)

Lord Jesus, you are mighty God and Prince of Peace: Lord, have mercy.

Lord Jesus, you are Son of God and Son of Mary: Christ, have mercy.

Lord Jesus, you are Word made flesh and splendour of the Father: Lord, have mercy.

Introduction to the Scripture Readings

Numbers 6:22-27 – The 'Blessing of Aaron' expresses God's care for humanity: a suitable New Year wish for all believers.

Galatians 4:4-7 – Because of the birth of Mary's child, we can all be called children of God.

Luke 2:16-21 – On the eighth day Mary's child was circumcised and given the name Jesus.

The General Intercessions *(Samples)*

Introduction *(by the Presider)*
God graciously blesses all of humanity, so we can bring forward our needs with confidence:

Intercessions *(announced by the deacon, cantor or another person)*

1.   That those who follow Christ may remain loyal and faithful throughout this New Year.
     (Pause for silent prayer)   Lord, hear us.

2.   That all who worship God – in churches, temples and mosques –
     may grow in respect and tolerance for each other.
     (Pause for silent prayer)   Lord, hear us.

3.   That we may continue to pray and work for peace, globally and locally.
     (Pause for silent prayer)   Lord, hear us.

4.   That mothers may learn from Mary the Mother of God
     to treasure every moment of their children's lives. *(Pause for silent prayer)*   Lord, hear us.

5.   That this New Year may bring fresh enthusiasm and strong growth to this community.
     (Pause for silent prayer)   Lord, hear us.

6.   That perpetual light may shine on all our dead,
     especially those taken from us in the last twelve months – whom we remember now...
     (Pause for silent prayer)   Lord, hear us.

Conclusion *(by the Presider)*
Gracious God, you bless your people with peace and justice:
Accept our prayers and give us your help, through Christ our Lord. Amen.

FOR LITURGY PLANNERS

Liturgical Suggestions

Penitential Rite c-iii. Preface of Christmas 2. Eucharistic Prayer 2. Solemn Blessing 3 (Beginning of the New Year) or 10 (Ordinary Time 1: The Blessing of Aaron – see First Reading)

Songs: Christmas Carols; 'When Creation Was Begun'; 'Lord of All Hopefulness'.

SECOND SUNDAY OF CHRISTMAS

FOR PRESIDERS

Opening Comment

We gather to celebrate the first Sunday of 2005, with thankfulness for the year just gone. We ask God for continuing care and protection as we face this New Year, not knowing what it will bring.

Penitential Rite: Confident that God's mercy has no end, we remember our sins: (pause)
Lord Jesus, you are mighty God and Prince of Peace: Lord, have mercy.
Lord Jesus, you are Son of God and Son of Mary: Christ, have mercy.
Lord Jesus, you are Word made flesh and splendour of the Father: Lord, have mercy.

Introduction to the Scripture Readings

Ecclesiasticus 24:1-2, 8-12 – Wisdom will pitch her tent among the chosen people, predicts the author of Ecclesiasticus. This saying came true when the Word became flesh in Jesus. We are reminded of this in the response to the psalm which follows.

Ephesians 1:3-6, 15-18 – As God's children, we are chosen to share in divine wisdom, a wisdom that reached its fullness in Christ.

John 1:1-18 – The Gospel of Christmas Day is repeated, to reinforce the simple yet profound message: The Word became flesh.

The General Intercessions *(Samples)*

> **Introduction** *(by the Presider)*
> Let us bring our prayers to God, who in Jesus was made flesh.
>
> **Intercessions** *(announced by the deacon, cantor or another person)*
> 1. For those who claim the name of Christian,
>   that they may accept the mystery of Jesus, human and divine.
>   *(Pause for silent prayer)*   Lord, hear us.
>
> 2. For the people for whom God seems distant and uncaring,
>   that they see the full beauty of God, revealed in Jesus. *(Pause for silent prayer)*   Lord, hear us.
>
> 3. For the nations where war and strife cause much suffering (especially N & N),
>   that this New Year may bring them peace. *(Pause for silent prayer)*   Lord, hear us.
>
> 4. For all of us, in this two thousand and fifth year of our Saviour,
>   that we may have the grace and courage to make a new start.
>   *(Pause for silent prayer)*   Lord, hear us.
>
> 5. For those who have died (especially N & N),
>   that perpetual light may shine on them. *(Pause for silent prayer)*   Lord, hear us.
>
> 6. For our own needs, which we remember quietly. *(Long pause for silent prayer)*   Lord, hear us.
>
> **Conclusion** *(by the Presider)*
> O God, your Word reveals your care and compassion:
> Receive the prayers we make, through Jesus Christ our Lord. Amen.

FOR LITURGY PLANNERS

Liturgical Suggestions

Penitential Rite c-iii. First Opening Prayer. Preface of Christmas 2. Eucharistic Prayer 3. Solemn Blessing 3 (New Year).

Songs: Christmas Carols; 'Christ be our Light'.

The Week Ahead

Thursday 6 January: The Epiphany of the Lord (Holyday of Obligation) is also called 'Three Kings Day'.
Friday 7 January (First Friday): Christmas Day is celebrated today in churches following the Julian Calendar (e.g. in Russia).
Sunday 9 January: Feast of the Baptism of the Lord. Might a baptism be celebrated during Mass?

THE EPIPHANY OF THE LORD

FOR PRESIDERS

Opening Comment

On this feast of the Epiphany we celebrate the revelation of who Christ is. The visit of the three wise men reminds us that Jesus came as the Saviour of all nations, including ours. We worship God who wants all people to be saved.

Penitential Rite: As we rejoice in God's forgiveness, let us call to mind our own need of divine mercy: (PAUSE)
Lord Jesus, you came to gather the nations into the peace of God's kingdom: Lord, have mercy.
You come in word and sacrament to strengthen us in holiness: Christ, have mercy.
You will come in glory with salvation for your people: Lord, have mercy.

Introduction to the Scripture Readings

Isaiah 60:1-6 – Isaiah refers to foreign people coming to worship the God of Israel, just as the three wise men did.
Ephesians 3:2-3, 5-6 – Paul talks about the meaning of the feast: in Jesus, salvation is made available to Jews and pagans alike.
Matthew 2:1-12 – The events celebrated on the Epiphany are described in the Gospel.

The General Intercessions (*Samples*)

Introduction (*by the Presider*)
Let us bring our prayers to God, who saves the poor when they cry out for help.

Intercessions (*announced by the deacon, cantor or another person*)

1. For the people of all the nations,
   that they may hear and believe the Good News of salvation.
   (Pause for silent prayer)   Lord, hear us.

2. For the Jewish people, our brothers and sisters,
   that through their faithfulness to God's word, they too may reach the Kingdom.
   (Pause for silent prayer)   Lord, hear us.

3. For people of all faiths and of none,
   that in this New Year they may grow in faith and love. *(Pause for silent prayer)* Lord, hear us.

4. For those in our midst who are sick or in sorrow,
   that our support may remind them of God's unfailing compassion.
   (Pause for silent prayer)   Lord, hear us.

5. For our friends and relatives who have died (especially N & N),
   that eternal salvation may be theirs. *(Pause for silent prayer)*   Lord, hear us.

6. For our own needs, for those who have asked our prayers...
   (Long pause for silent prayer)   Lord, hear us.

Conclusion (*by the Presider*)
O God, you rule the earth with justice:
Help us according to our needs, we pray, through Christ our Lord. Amen.

FOR LITURGY PLANNERS

Liturgical Suggestions

Epiphany is a feast of light: make sure all available candles are alight for Masses today. Use incense today as at Christmas. Penitential Rite c-ii. First Opening Prayer. Preface of Epiphany. Eucharistic Prayer 1 (with special form of *In union with the whole Church*). Solemn Blessing 4 (Epiphany). The Epiphany announcement of the great feasts and holy days of 2005 may be made during Mass or in the newsletter: for official text, please see *The Liturgical Calendar 2005*.

Songs: Christmas Carols; 'We Three Kings of Orient Are'; 'Praise the Lord all you nations'.

THE BAPTISM OF THE LORD

FOR PRESIDERS

Opening Comment

This feast of the Baptism of the Lord marks the last day of Christmas. At his baptism Jesus sees how much he is loved by God and is given the power to go out and spread the news. We share that power through our baptism.

Penitential Rite: We begin now by blessing water and recalling our own baptism...
(Replace usual formula with the Rite of Blessing and Sprinkling Holy Water – see **Roman Missal** pp. 387 to 389)
OR
Penitential Rite: To begin, let us remember the areas of darkness in our own lives, made clear by God's healing light (pause):
You raise the dead to life in the Spirit: Lord, have mercy.
You bring pardon and peace to the sinner: Christ, have mercy.
You bring light to those in darkness: Lord, have mercy.

Introduction to the Scripture Readings

Isaiah 42: 1-4, 6-7 – Christians idenitfy the servant described by Isaiah with Christ and the Church.
Acts 10: 34-38 – Peter recalls how Jesus was anointed with the Holy Spirit, and the difference that made.
Matthew 3:13-17 – The events celebrated in today's feast are described by St Matthew.

The General Intercessions *(Samples)*

Introduction *(by the Presider)*
Let us bring our prayers to God, who is full of majesty and power and splendour.

Intercessions *(announced by the deacon, cantor or another person)*

1.   For all the baptised,
     that they may take their Christian commitment seriously. *(Pause for silent prayer)*   Lord, hear us.

2.   For newborn babies, and all who will soon be baptised,
     that they may have the grace to live truly Christian lives. *(Pause for silent prayer)*   Lord, hear us.

3.   For those preparing for Confirmation this year,
     that they may be filled with the Holy Spirit. *(Pause for silent prayer)*   Lord, hear us.

4.   For the elderly and all who are lonely,
     that they may know our support these January days. *(Pause for silent prayer)*   Lord, hear us.

5.   For our friends and relatives who have died (especially N & N),
     that they may enter the presence of the Lord. *(Pause for silent prayer)*   Lord, hear us.

6.   For our own needs, for those who have asked for prayers...
     (Long pause for silent prayer)   Lord, hear us.

Conclusion *(by the Presider)*
O God, you rule the earth with justice,
Help us all according to our needs, through Christ our Lord. Amen.

FOR LITURGY PLANNERS

Liturgical Suggestions

Celebrate baptism during Mass today, or at least bless and sprinkle Holy Water at the start of Mass. If rite of sprinking is omitted, use Penitential Rite c-v. First Opening Prayer. Preface of the Baptism of the Lord. Eucharistic Prayer 2. Solemn Blessing 4 (Epiphany) or 10 (Ordinary Time 1).

• *Rite for celebrating Baptism during Mass: Opening dialogue and signing with the Sign of the Cross at the door is followed by Entrance Procession and Gloria. Opening Prayer, then readings of the day and homily. The celebration of baptism is next, with Mass then continuing as normal, and special blessing prayers of Baptism added to Concluding Rite. (Beforehand: celebrate preparatory rites by blessing water and, possibly, anoint with oil of catechumens.)*

Songs: Christmas Carols; 'Here I am Lord'; 'Come to the Water'; 'Holy God We Praise Thy Name'.

The Week Ahead

Tuesday 11 January: International Thank-You Day.
Saturday 15 January: St Ita of Limerick, foster-mother of the saints of Ireland, is honoured.

SECOND SUNDAY IN ORDINARY TIME

FOR PRESIDERS

Opening Comment

The Christmas Season ended last Sunday, but the season of Lent begins very early this year, on 9 February. During the short time between the two seasons, we celebrate the Sundays of Ordinary Time, learning a little more each week about the life of Jesus.

Penitential Rite To prepare ourselves for this celebration, let us call to mind our sins: (pause)
Lord Jesus, you raise us to new life: Lord, have mercy.
Lord Jesus, you forgive us our sins: Christ, have mercy.
Lord Jesus, you feed us with your body and blood: Lord, have mercy.

Introduction to the Scripture Readings

Isaiah 49:3, 5-6 – God's Chosen One will bring salvation to all peoples.
1 Corinthians 1:1-3 – Includes the very start of Paul's first letter to the people of Corinth; we'll be reading from that letter each week until the start of Lent in early February.
John 1:29-34 – John the Baptist introduces Jesus to us as the Lamb of God, the Chosen One.

The General Intercessions *(Samples)*

Introduction *(by the Presider)*
Let us raise our prayers to God, who stoops down to hear us.

Intercessions *(announced by the deacon, cantor or another person)*

1.	For all the members of the Church, we pray. *(Pause for silent prayer)*	Lord, hear us.
2.	For those preparing for baptism, confirmation or First Communion, we pray. *(Pause for silent prayer)*	Lord, hear us.
3.	For all who suffer because of war or famine, we pray. *(Pause for silent prayer)*	Lord, hear us.
4.	For those who are ill, at home or in hospitals or nursing homes, we pray. *(Pause for silent prayer)*	Lord, hear us.
5.	For our people who have died (especially N & N), we pray. *(Pause for silent prayer)*	Lord, hear us.
6.	For our own needs, we pray... *(Long pause for silent prayer)*	Lord, hear us.

Conclusion *(by the Presider)*
Lord our God, we proclaim your justice and mercy;
Hear the prayers we make in faith, through Christ our Lord. Amen.

FOR LITURGY PLANNERS

Liturgical Suggestions

Penitential Rite c-vi. Alternative Opening Prayer. The intercessions provided are short; encourage people to pray silently before the 'Lord, hear us' is said (on this and every Sunday). Preface of Sundays in Ordinary Time 1. Eucharistic Prayer 3. Solemn Blessing 11 (Ordinary Time 2).

Songs: 'Ag Críost an Síol'; 'Holy God We Praise thy Name'; 'Lord of All Hopefulness'.

The Week Ahead

Monday 17 January: Martin Luther King Jr Day in the USA and Switzerland.
Tuesday 18 January: Week of Prayer for Christian Unity runs from today until Tuesday 25.
Friday 21 January: Id al Adha (Feast of the Sacrifice) is celebrated by the Islam world.

THIRD SUNDAY IN ORDINARY TIME

FOR PRESIDERS

Opening Comment
This Sunday falls within the annual Week of Prayer for Christian Unity, when the Church prays that all Christians may grow closer together. As we join with Christians all over the world today to honour the death and resurrection of Jesus, we pray that the journey to full unity may soon be complete.
  Penitential Rite: We have not always worked for peace and unity. We acknowledge our own sins: (pause)
  I confess...

Introduction to the Scripture Readings
Isaiah 8:23 to 9:3 – A prophecy of the time when the light of the world is to come, a prophecy Christians see fulfilled in Jesus.
1 Corinthians 1:10-13, 17 – Paul's appeal against the splintering of the community fits well with the themes of the Week of Prayer for Christian Unity.
Matthew 4:12-23 – The Gospel describes the visit of Jesus to places on the fringes of Israel, just as the prophet Isaiah had foretold.

The General Intercessions (*Samples*)

Introduction (*by the Presider*)
The Lord is our light and our help, so let us bring all our needs to God.

Intercessions (*announced by the deacon, cantor or another person*)

1.	For a passion for unity among all who follow Christ, we pray. (*Pause for silent prayer*)	Lord, hear us.
2.	For harmony among nations and the defeat of violence, we pray. (*Pause for silent prayer*)	Lord, hear us.
3.	For the gift of hope and light to all who feel lost, we pray. (*Pause for silent prayer*)	Lord, hear us.
4.	For the healing and strength of those who suffer, we pray. (*Pause for silent prayer*)	Lord, hear us.
5.	For eternal life for the dead (especially N & N), we pray. (*Pause for silent prayer*)	Lord, hear us.
6.	For our own needs, we pray... (*Long pause for silent prayer*)	Lord, hear us.

Conclusion (*by the Presider*)
O Lord, our light and our help, you refresh our hope and give us fresh heart:
Grant our prayers, we pray, through Christ our Lord. Amen.

FOR LITURGY PLANNERS

Liturgical Suggestions
Penitential Rite a. Alternative Opening Prayer. Gospel – full form. Preface of Christian Unity (Roman Missal page 479) or Preface of Sundays 4. Eucharistic Prayer 1. Solemn Blessing 12 (Ordinary Time 3).

Songs: 'Be not Afraid'; 'Here I am, Lord'; 'City of God'.

The Week Ahead
Monday 25 January: Week of Prayer for Christian Unity ends today. Tu B'Shevat (New Year of Trees) in Israel.
Tuesday 26 January: Australia Day (Australia). Republic Day (India).
Wednesday 27 January: WWII Genocide Memorial Day.
Friday 28 January: St Thomas Aquinas, patron of schools, universities, students and booksellers.

FOURTH SUNDAY IN ORDINARY TIME

FOR PRESIDERS

Opening Comment
We gather to celebrate the resurrection of our Saviour and to remember his beautiful teachings. In the beatitudes, which we read today, Jesus describe the kinds of people who are blessed in God's eyes. We hope to join the company of all these saints in the heavenly liturgy.

> *Penitential Rite: Jesus has shown us the way to walk: let us remember when we sought other paths: (pause)*
> Lord Jesus, you have shown us the way to the Father: Lord, have mercy.
> Lord Jesus, you have given us the consolation of the truth: Christ, have mercy.
> Lord Jesus, you are the Good Shepherd, leading us into everlasting life: Lord, have mercy.

Introduction to the Scripture Readings
Zephaniah 2:3, 3:12-13 – Zephaniah describes the kind of people who find favour with God.
1 Corinthians 1:26-31 – Paul reminds us that we are to rely not on our own efforts, but on God's power.
Matthew 5:1-12 – Today we begin to read from a section in Matthew's Gospel which describes the Sermon on the Mount.

The General Intercessions *(Samples)*

Introduction *(by the Presider)*
We bring our prayers to God, who raises up all who are bowed down.

Intercessions *(announced by the deacon, cantor or another person)*

1. That those who suffer persecution for their faith may receive strength and courage, we pray. *(Pause for silent prayer)*   Lord, hear us.

2. That the people who hunger and thirst for justice may see it come to pass, we pray. *(Pause for silent prayer)*   Lord, hear us.

3. That peacemakers may succeed in ending hatred between people and nations, we pray. *(Pause for silent prayer)*   Lord, hear us.

4. That those suffering from illness may know the healing power of God, we pray. *(Pause for silent prayer)*   Lord, hear us.

5. That all who mourn may experience comfort, we pray. *(Pause for silent prayer)*   Lord, hear us.

6. That those who have died may receive a great reward in heaven (especially N & N), we pray. *(Pause for silent prayer)*   Lord, hear us.

Conclusion *(by the Presider)*
Lord our God, you keep faith with people in any kind of need:
Hear the prayer we make to you, through Christ our Lord. Amen.

FOR LITURGY PLANNERS

Liturgical Suggestions
Penitential Rite c-vii. Alternative Opening Prayer. Preface of Sundays in Ordinary Time 8 and Eucharistic Prayer 3, or Eucharistic Prayer 4 with its own preface. Solemn Blessing 10 (Ordinary Time 1).

Songs: Any song based on the Beatitudes, or 'Be Thou My Vision'; 'Ag Críost an Síol'.

The Week Ahead
Tuesday 1 February: St Brigid is honoured, on the first day of spring.
Wednesday 2 February: Candles are blessed on the feast of the Presentation of the Lord (Candlemas). Also 'Groundhog Day'.
Thursday 3 February: The newly-blessed candles are used to bless throats on the feast of St Blaise.
Friday 4 February (First Friday).

FEAST OF ST BLAISE

FOR PRESIDERS

Opening Comment

Today we remember St Blaise, who was a bishop in Armenia over 1,500 years ago. Before dying as a martyr, he is said to have saved a child from choking. He is venerated as the patron of those who suffer diseases of the throat.

> *Penitential Rite As we prepare to celebrate the healing power of God, let us acknowledge our need of divine help: (pause)*
> Lord Jesus, you healed the sick: Lord, have mercy.
> Lord Jesus, you forgave sinners: Christ have mercy.
> Lord Jesus, you gave us yourself to heal us and bring us strength: Lord, have mercy.

Introduction to the Scripture Readings

Romans 5:1-5 – Suffering can bring us many gifts from God, including patience, perseverance and hope.
Mark 16:15-20 – Jesus promises that in his name believers will lay their hands on the sick and they will recover.

The General Intercessions *(Samples)*

Introduction *(by the Presider)*
Strong is God's love for us, so we bring forward our needs on this feast of St Blaise:

Intercessions *(announced by the deacon, cantor or another person)*

1. That all who carry the cross of suffering may realise that Christ is with them.
   (Pause for silent prayer)   Lord, hear us.

2. That those who suffer from sickness and disease may experience healing.
   (Pause for silent prayer)   Lord, hear us.

3. That the mentally ill and their families may find peace and new strength.
   (Pause for silent prayer)   Lord, hear us.

4. That doctors and nurses and all who care for the sick may show patience and sensitivity.
   (Pause for silent prayer)   Lord, hear us.

5. That those who suffer from ailments of the throat may enjoy relief, at St Blaise's intercession.
   (Pause for silent prayer)   Lord, hear us.

6. That God may help each of us, according to our needs...
   (Long pause for silent prayer)   Lord, hear us.

Conclusion *(by the Presider)*
Faithful God, you show your love by supporting your people in sickness and in health:
Hear our prayers for healing – and grant them, through Christ our Lord. Amen.

FOR LITURGY PLANNERS

Liturgical Suggestions

Penitential Rite c-viii. Opening prayer from the Proper of Saints (3 February). Other Mass prayers from Common of Pastors: (4) for bishops (page 716-717). Preface of Pastors, or from Anointing of the Sick: Anointing within Mass (in *Pastoral Care of the Sick*, Veritas Publications, 1982, page 114.). Eucharistic Prayer 2. Prayer over the People 26 (Feasts of Saints). The blessing of throats (using candles blessed at Mass on 2 February) is given after the Gospel of the Mass. Choose from these formulae:
Through the intercession of St Blaise, bishop and martyr, may God deliver you from all ailments of the throat and from every other evil. In the name of the Father, ✠ and of the Son, and of the Holy Spirit. Amen.
or
Through the intercession of St Blaise, bishop and martyr, may God deliver you from every disease of the throat and from every other illness. In the name of the Father, ✠ and of the Son, and of the Holy Spirit. Amen.

Songs: 'Lay Your Hands Gently Upon Us'; 'Only in God'; 'Be Still and Know that I am God'.

FIFTH SUNDAY IN ORDINARY TIME

FOR PRESIDERS

Opening Comment

This is the last Sunday before Lent, which is celebrated as Temperance Sunday. In the liturgy, we hear that we are the salt of the earth and the light of the world. Rejoicing in this calling, we praise God who sustains us all our days.

Penitential Rite: Though we are called to be light, sometimes we have chosen darkness.
Let us remember our sins: (pause)
Lord Jesus, you raise us to new life: Lord, have mercy.
Lord Jesus, you forgive us our sins: Christ, have mercy.
Lord Jesus, you feed us with your body and blood: Lord, have mercy.

Introduction to the Scripture Readings

Isaiah 58: 7-10 – Isaiah suggests some ways of living a good life.
1 Corinthians 2:1-5 – In Paul's letter to the people of Corinth, he speaks of his reliance on the power of God.
Matthew 5:13-16 – Jesus calls us to be examples of Christian living.

The General Intercessions *(Samples)*

Introduction *(by the Presider)*
Let us bring our prayers to the Lord, in whom we place our trust.

Intercessions *(announced by the deacon, cantor or another person)*

1.   For Christians, that their example of right living may light up the world,
     we pray. *(Pause for silent prayer)*   Lord, hear us.

2.   For the exploited and oppressed, that they may be set free,
     we pray. *(Pause for silent prayer)*   Lord, hear us.

3   For the hungry and homeless, that the wealthy may learn to share with them,
     we pray. *(Pause for silent prayer)*   Lord, hear us.

4.   For those who bear the cross, that their sufferings may not wear them out,
     we pray. *(Pause for silent prayer)*   Lord, hear us.

5.   For all who find temperance difficult, that our prayers may support them in their struggle,
     we pray. *(Pause for silent prayer)*   Lord, hear us.

6   For those who have died,
     (especially N & N who died recently and N & N whose anniversaries occur),
     that they may praise God forever in heaven,
     we pray. *(Pause for silent prayer)*   Lord, hear us.

Conclusion *(by the Presider)*
O God, you are the light that makes clear our way before us:
Listen to the prayers we make, through Christ our Lord. Amen.

FOR LITURGY PLANNERS

Liturgical Suggestions

Penitential Rite c-vi. First Opening Prayer. Preface of Sundays in Ordinary Time 1 and Eucharistic Prayer 2, or Eucharistic Prayer 4 with its own preface (which may not be used again until June). Solemn Blessing 12 (Ordinary Time 3).

Songs: 'Let us Build the City of God'; 'Glory and Praise to Our God'; Walk in the Light'.

The Week Ahead

Tuesday 8 February: Shrove or Pancake Tuesday, the last day of 'Carnival' (Mardi Gras).
Wednesday 9 February: Ash Wednesday, a day of fast and abstinence. Also Chinese New Year's Day (Year of the Rooster).
Thursday 10 February: Hijra New Year (Islam).
Friday 11 February: World Day of the Sick (Our Lady of Lourdes/St Gobnait).

ASH WEDNESDAY

FOR PRESIDERS

Opening Comment
Welcome to the season of Lent. Today we begin the journey of penance and reflection that will bring us to the celebration of the passion, death and resurrection of Jesus at Easter time.
Let us pray for the grace to keep Lent faithfully...
(Pause for silent prayer: the Opening Prayer follows immediately.)

Introduction to the Scripture Readings
Joel 2:12-18 – A call to the community to turn back to the Lord, fasting and asking for mercy.
2 Corinthians 5:20 to 6:2 – Paul's message is clear: now is the time to be reconciled to God.
Mathew 6:1-6, 16-18 – Jesus invites his followers to be converted in their hearts, and warns them against 'making a show of themselves'!

The Blessing and Giving of Ashes follows the Gospel (or homily) *see Roman Missal, pp 74-75.*

The General Intercessions *(Samples)*

> **Introduction** *(by the Presider)*
> Brothers and sisters, our God is full of mercy and compassion, so let us ask for divine help:
>
> **Intercessions** *(announced by the deacon, cantor or another person)*

1	That all who are signed with ashes today may turn back to God during this holy season. *(Pause for silent prayer)*	Lord, hear us.
2	That those who have grown lukewarm may find new enthusiasm in their faith. *(Pause for silent prayer)*	Lord, hear us.
3.	That people in need throughout the world may benefit from our lenten practices. *(Pause for silent prayer)*	Lord, hear us.
4.	That, during this season, we may learn to set our own interests aside and work for the good of others. *(Pause for silent prayer)*	Lord, hear us.
5.	That God may send help for all our needs, particularly those we remember now... *(Long pause for silent prayer)*	Lord, hear us.

> **Conclusion** *(by the Presider)*
> God of mercy and compassion, you cleanse us and give us your help:
> Hear the prayers your people make in faith, through Christ our Lord. Amen.

FOR LITURGY PLANNERS

Liturgical Suggestions
The church is bare of flowers or other ornaments today: everything looks 'lenten'. The penitential rite is replaced by the blessing and giving of ashes (after the Gospel). If this is not possible because of time constraints, simply celebrate a Liturgy of the Word (with the readings of the day) followed by a service of ashes.
If Mass is celebrated: Preface of Lent 4, Eucharistic Prayer 2, simple final blessing.

Songs: 'God of Mercy and Compassion'; 'Renew your Hearts'; 'Praise to the Holiest'.

FIRST SUNDAY OF LENT

FOR PRESIDERS

Opening Comment
We celebrate the first Sunday of Lent. All over the world today, men and women are beginning a period of preparation for their baptism at the Easter Vigil. Like them, we spend Lent preparing to renew our baptismal vows at Easter, looking forward to our blessing with Easter water and to receiving the gift of a new start.

Penitential Rite: Aware that God's grace within us brings us to repentance, let us call to mind our sins… (pause)
You were sent to heal the contrite: Lord, have mercy.
You came to call sinners: Christ, have mercy.
You plead for us at the right hand of the Father: Lord, have mercy.

Introduction to the Scripture Readings
Genesis 2:7-9, 3:1-7 – Describes the entry of sin into the world, through the story of Adam and Eve.
Romans 5:12-19 – Paul brings the First Reading and Gospel together, and tells us that the death of Jesus freed all from sin.
Matthew 4:1-11 – The Gospel shows us that even Jesus had to endure temptation.

The General Intercessions *(Samples)*

Introduction *(by the Presider)*
As we begin the lenten journey, let us remember all those in need:

Intercessions *(announced by the deacon, cantor or another person)*

1.   For Pope N, our Bishop N and all our leaders in faith,
     we pray. *(Pause for silent prayer)*   Lord, hear us.

2.   For peace and reconciliation in our country and throughout the world,
     we pray. *(Pause for silent prayer)*   Lord, hear us.

3.   For the hungry, the poor, the homeless,
     we pray. *(Pause for silent prayer)*   Lord, hear us.

4.   For this community, particularly for our friends who are ill,
     we pray. *(Pause for silent prayer)*   Lord, hear us.

5.   For those who have died,
     (especially N & N who died recently and N & N whose anniversaries occur)
     we pray. *(Pause for silent prayer)*   Lord, hear us.

6.   For all our own needs and intentions,
     we pray… *(Long pause for silent prayer)*   Lord, hear us.

Conclusion *(by the Presider)*
O God, you understand our weakness, you know our needs:
Give us the joy of your help, we beseech you, through Christ our Lord. Amen.

FOR LITURGY PLANNERS

Liturgical Suggestions
Penitential Rite c-i. No Gloria today, no Alleluia, no flowers. First Opening Prayer. Shorter form of second reading (Romans 5:12, 17-19). Preface of the First Sunday of Lent. Eucharistic Prayer 3. Prayer over the People 24, preceded by the invitation 'Bow your heads and pray for God's blessing', and followed by the simple blessing: 'And may almighty God bless you, the Father, ✠ and the Son, and the Holy Spirit'.

Songs:
'Praise to the Holiest'; 'Be Not Afraid'; 'Renew your Hearts'.

The Week Ahead
Monday 14 February: St Valentine's Day (also Sts Cyril & Methodius, Patrons of Europe).
Tuesday 15 February: National Flag Day (Canada).
Friday 18 February: Anniversary of the death of Martin Luther (at the age of 62, in 1546).
Saturday 19 February: Ashara (Islam) is a Shi'a holiday, marking the martyrdom of Imam Hussein.

SECOND SUNDAY OF LENT

FOR PRESIDERS

Opening Comment
Now that we are ten days into the season of Lent, our goal is clarified in today's liturgy. The Gospel of the Transfiguration reminds us that we are destined for glory. Like the disciples, we keep this glimpse of glory in our hearts in the dark days ahead. Resurrection will follow, as surely as day follows night.
Penitential Rite: As we begin the second week of our lenten journey, we ask for pardon and strength.
Let us call to mind our need of God's grace (pause):
I confess...

Introduction to the Scripture Readings
Genesis 12:1-4 – God's promise to Abram who became Abraham is described.
2 Timothy 1:8-10 – Paul reminds us that God is on our side, that Jesus rose from the dead for us.
Matthew 17:1-9 – The Gospel gives a glimpse of the glory promised to Jesus after his death and resurrection.

The General Intercessions *(Samples)*

Introduction *(by the Presider)*
Let us bring our prayers to God, who loves justice and right.

Intercessions *(announced by the deacon, cantor or another person)*

1.   For all the members of the Church, as they continue on their lenten journey, we pray. *(Pause for silent prayer)* Lord, hear us.

2.   For children and adults preparing to become members of the Church at Easter time, we pray. *(Pause for silent prayer)* Lord, hear us.

3.   For the Jewish people, the sons and daughters of Abraham, we pray. *(Pause for silent prayer)* Lord, hear us.

4.   For those who are starving in a world of plenty, we pray. *(Pause for silent prayer)* Lord, hear us.

5.   For this community, and particularly for those who are lonely or fearful, we pray. *(Pause for silent prayer)* Lord, hear us.

6.   For those who have gone before us in faith (especially N & N who died recently and N & N whose anniversaries occur), we pray. *(Pause for silent prayer)* Lord, hear us.

Conclusion *(by the Presider)*
O Lord, you look with kindness on those who revere you:
Give us your help, for all our hope is in you.
We make our prayer through Christ our Lord. Amen.

FOR LITURGY PLANNERS

Liturgical Suggestions
Penitential Rite a. First Opening Prayer. Preface of the Second Sunday of Lent. Eucharistic Prayer 1.
Prayer over the People 4, preceded by the invitation 'Bow your heads and pray for God's blessing', and followed by the simple blessing: 'And may almighty God bless you, the Father, ✠ and the Son, and the Holy Spirit'.

Songs: 'Be Thou My Vision'; 'May Your Love Be Upon Us O Lord'; 'Christ be Our Light'.

The Week Ahead
Monday 21 February: President's Day is celebrated in the US, jointly honouring the birthdays of George Washington (12 February) and Abraham Lincoln (22 February).
Tuesday 22 February: The Chair of St Peter ('Ancestor Day' in pre-Christian Rome).
Thursday 23 February: 'Defenders of the Motherland' Day (Russia).

THIRD SUNDAY OF LENT

FOR PRESIDERS

Opening Comment
Today's readings about water and thirst remind us that this is a baptismal season. During Lent, many people all over the world look forward to their baptism, while those already baptised prepare to renew their promises.

Penitential Rite: To prepare ourselves for this celebration, let us call to mind our sins: (pause)

Lord Jesus, you came to reconcile us to one another and to the Father: Lord, have mercy.

Lord Jesus, you heal the wounds of sin and division: Christ, have mercy.

Lord Jesus, you intercede for us with your Father: Lord, have mercy.

Introduction to the Scripture Readings
Exodus 17:3-7 – A thirsty people complain to Moses, and God gives them water from the rock.

Romans 5:1-2, 5-8 – A reflection on God's love, which was proved, Paul says, by Jesus' death on the cross.

John 4:5-42 – The Gospel story of the woman at the well contains the promise of living water to those who believe, foreshadowed in the reading from Exodus.

The General Intercessions *(Samples)*

Introduction *(by the Presider)*
Let us come before the Lord, bringing forward all our needs.

Intercessions *(announced by the deacon, cantor or another person)*

1. For the baptised,
    that they may appreciate the gifts that are theirs. *(Pause for silent prayer)*   Lord, hear us.

2. For adults and children preparing for baptism,
    that in our prayer and support we may encourage them. *(Pause for silent prayer)* Lord, hear us.

3. For all who thirst for meaning and truth,
    that they may experience God's revealing grace. *(Pause for silent prayer)*   Lord, hear us.

4. For poor nations, where water is scarce,
    that they may have the help they need in the fight against thirst.
    (Pause for silent prayer)   Lord, hear us.

5. For this community, and particularly for people in any kind of difficulty,
    that this Lent may teach us to be true friends of those in need.
    (Pause for silent prayer)   Lord, hear us.

6. For those who have died (especially N & N),
    that their thirst for life without end may be satisfied. *(Pause for silent prayer)*   Lord, hear us.

Conclusion *(by the Presider)*
O God, we are yours, you lead us by the hand:
Send the help we need, we pray, through Christ our Lord. Amen

FOR LITURGY PLANNERS

Liturgical Suggestions
Penitential Rite c-iv – or replace penitential rite with Blessing and Sprinking of Holy Water (formula a or b.) Alternative Opening Prayer. Shorter form of Gospel (John 4:5-15, 19-26, 39-42). Preface of the Third Sunday of Lent. Eucharistic Prayer 2. Prayer over the People 13, preceded by the invitation: *'Bow your heads and pray for God's blessing'*, and followed by the simple blessing: *'And may almighty God bless you, the Father,* ✠ *and the Son, and the Holy Spirit'*.

Songs: 'Praise to the Holiest'; Like The Deer That Yearns'; 'Lord Of All Hopefulness'.

The Week Ahead
Tuesday 1 March: St David, the patron saint of Wales, is honoured today. Also International Women of Colour Day.

Wednesday 2 March: Anniversary of the death of John Wesley (at 88, in 1791).

Friday 4 March (First Friday): Women's World Day of Prayer.

• Next Sunday, the Fourth Sunday of Lent, is celebrated as Mothering Sunday or Mother's Day in Ireland and Britain.

FOURTH SUNDAY OF LENT

FOR PRESIDERS

Opening Comment
Traditionally, this Sunday is called Laetare Sunday, which means 'a day for joy'. Lent is half over, and the celebration of the death and resurrection of Jesus is nearer. At this midpoint of Lent, it is traditional to honour mothers, treasuring those still with us and praying for those we have lost to death.
> *Penitential Rite: Let us remember the love we have experienced in our lives*
> *and call to mind the times we failed to show love: (pause)*
> I confess...

Introduction to the Scripture Readings
Samuel 16:1, 6-7, 10-13 – God's choice of the young boy Samuel is described in the first reading.
Ephesians 5:8-14 – The second reading and Gospel both reflect on light and darkness, and the new sight that believers can have.
John 9:1-41 – The healing of the man born blind is described: believers also need to go from blindness to new sight.

The General Intercessions *(Samples)*

Introduction *(by the Presider)*
Brothers and sisters, let us turn to God for help.

Intercessions *(announced by the deacon, minister or member of the Faithful)*

1. For the Church,
   that it may be a sign of light and hope. *(Pause for silent prayer)*   Lord, hear us.

2. For those responsible for the common good,
   that they may work hard on behalf of everyone, especially the weak.
   (Pause for silent prayer)   Lord, hear us.

3. For all who experience the sufferings of life,
   that they may not be crushed by temptation. *(Pause for silent prayer)*   Lord, hear us.

4. For people afflicted by blindness or limited sight,
   that they may benefit from our sensitivity and support. *(Pause for silent prayer)*   Lord, hear us.

5. For the mothers of this community, and for all who care for children,
   that joy may be theirs, in this life and the next. *(Pause for silent prayer)*   Lord, hear us.

6. For mothers who have died, and for all the dead (especially N & N),
   that they may dwell in God's house forever. *(Pause for silent prayer)*   Lord, hear us.

Conclusion *(by the Presider)*
God, source of forgiveness, in Jesus you have given us freedom of heart:
Hear our prayers and help us to do your will, through Christ our Lord. Amen.

FOR LITURGY PLANNERS

Liturgical Suggestions
Today is Laetare Sunday (Mothers' Day). Rose vestments may be worn, or the altar area may be decorated with a rose-coloured cloth or flowers. Penitential Rite a). Alternative Opening Prayer. Shorter form of Gospel (John 9:1, 6-9, 13-17, 34-36). Preface of the Fourth Sunday of Lent. Eucharistic Prayer 3. Prayer over the People 23, preceded by the invitation: *'Bow your heads and pray for God's blessing'*, and followed by the simple blessing: *'And may almighty God bless you, the Father, ✠ and the Son, and the Holy Spirit'.*

Songs: 'Amazing Grace'; 'Christ Be Our Light'; 'Grant To Us O Lord'.

The Week Ahead
Tuesday 8 March: International Women's Day is celebrated.
Saturday 12 March: Employee Day (USA).

FIFTH SUNDAY OF LENT

FOR PRESIDERS

Opening Comment

In just over ten days time, on Holy Thursday evening, the Easter Triduum will begin. The time when baptism is celebrated is now very close. We ask God's help for all the adults and children preparing for baptism this Easter, and pray that we may be fit and ready to renew our baptismal vows at the same feast.

Penitential Rite: To prepare ourselves to hear God's challenging word today,
let us call to mind our need of divine assistance: (pause)
You raise the dead to life in the Spirit: Lord, have mercy.
You bring pardon and peace to the sinner: Lord, have mercy.
You bring light to those in darkness: Lord, have mercy.

Introduction to the Scripture Readings

The three readings today focus on the question: 'How do we obtain life?'
Ezekiel 37: 12-14 – Ezekiel believes that those committed to God will find life after they die.
Romans 8:8-11 – Paul writes that through the Spirit we can find life.
John 11: 1-45 – The Gospel describes the raising of Lazarus and shows that all God's power is found in Jesus, who brings believers the fullness of life.

The General Intercessions (*Samples*)

Introduction (*by the Presider*)
Brothers and sisters, with trust we bring our prayers to the Father.

Intercessions (*announced by the deacon, minister or member of the Faithful*)

1.	That all Christians may firmly believe in life beyond the grave. (*Pause for silent prayer*)	Lord, hear us.
2.	That people plagued by doubts may be inspired by the Word of God. (*Pause for silent prayer*)	Lord, hear us.
3.	That those preparing to celebrate baptism this Easter may begin a full, new life in Christ. (*Pause for silent prayer*)	Lord, hear us.
4.	That all of us taking part in this celebration may receive strength to grow daily in the Christian life. (*Pause for silent prayer*)	Lord, hear us.
5.	That those who suffer because the one they love has died may know the compassion of Christ, who wept at the death of Lazarus. (*Pause for silent prayer*)	Lord, hear us.
6	That all the faithful departed (especially N & N) may meet Christ, the resurrection and the life. (*Pause for silent prayer*)	Lord, hear us.

Conclusion (*by the Presider*)
Heavenly Father, receive our prayers, and fill our hearts with your mercy,
so that safeguarding the gifts received through your goodness, we may walk in newness of life,
through Christ our Lord. Amen.

FOR LITURGY PLANNERS

Liturgical Suggestions

Penitential rite c-v, or replace with the Blessing and Sprinkling of Holy Water, formula a or b. Shorter form of Gospel (John 11:3-7, 17, 20-27, 33-45). Preface of the Fifth Sunday of Lent. Eucharistic Prayer 2. Solemn Blessing 5 (The Passion of the Lord).

Songs: 'I am the Bread of Life'; 'The Lord's my Shepherd'; 'Praise to the Holiest'.

The Week Ahead

Thursday 17 March: St Patrick's Day (Holyday of Obligation in Ireland).
Saturday 19 March: St Joseph. He is a patron of Belgium, Canada and Mexico – and of the Church, fathers and a happy death.
• Next Sunday is Palm Sunday.

COMMUNAL PENANCE SERVICE
FOR LENT 2005

Preparations
All priests taking part vest in alb and purple stole beforehand. Candles are lit: the church lights may be dimmed. Servers lead the entrance procession during the entrance song.

INTRODUCTORY RITES

Entrance Song (e.g. 'The Lord's My Shepherd' or 'O The Love of My Lord' or 'Lay your Hands Gently upon Us'.)

Greeting (e.g. The Lord be with you...)

Opening Comment *(by the Presider)*
'Welcome to this celebration of God's forgiveness, and of our reconciliation with God and one another. Our service has four parts. After this brief introduction (the first part), we will listen to God's word and reflect on it. Then we will celebrate the Rite of Reconciliation, during which everyone will have the opportunity of going to Confession. The service will end with an Act of Thanksgiving.
Let us pray...

Opening Prayer
(from the Rite of Penance*, choose from pages 115-117) Example:
Lord,
turn to us in mercy
and forgive us all our sins
that we may serve you in true freedom.
We ask this through Christ our Lord.
Amen.

LITURGY OF THE WORD

A selection of readings is given in the Rite of Penance*, pages 119 to 202. One reading may be sufficient – the healing of the man born blind (Fourth Sunday of Lent) or the raising of Lazarus (Fifth Sunday of Lent).

*The **homily** follows. See homily resources for the Fourth or Fifth Sunday of Lent in any publication.*

*The **examination of conscience** may take the form of a period of silence following the homily.*

Or the following may be used:
'We are called to be reconciled to God and to each other':
1. Reflecting on my relationship with God:
   Do I keep God's laws and commandments?
   Do I pray each day?
   Do I attend Mass when I should?
2. Reflecting on my relationship with others:
   What kind of person am I to live with? Am I kind to those around me, helpful and sensitive?
   What kind of person am I to work with? Am I honest?
   What kind of friend am I? Am I loyal and trustworthy?

Let us pause a moment to call to mind our own sins...
(A long pause for silent reflection follows)

COMMUNAL PENANCE SERVICE
FOR LENT 2005

RITE OF RECONCILIATION

Confession of sins

'Let us confess our sinfulness to God and one another:
I confess…'

A *litany of repentance* may be prayed (e.g. Rite of Penance* p. 239) or a song may be sung: e.g. 'God of Mercy and Compassion' or a version of the **Kyrie** (e.g. Lord Jesus, you came to reconcile us to one another and to the Father: Lord, have mercy… etc.)

The **Lord's Prayer** follows.

Individual confessions

(As the priests take up their positions, standing in various locations around the church, the presider explains the procedure.)
'You are now invited to make your Confession to the priest of your choice. Begin by saying to him:
"I am sorry for all my sins, especially for…"
Tell him your sins, listen to his advice and the penance he gives you, and hear him absolve your sins. Then return to your seat and pray for those still waiting to confess. When everyone has been absolved, we will pray together in thanksgiving.'

The presider may add:
I invite you to pray the Act of Sorrow:
'O my God, I am sorry for all my sins,
For not loving others and not loving you.
Help me to live like Jesus and not sin again.
Amen.'

THANKSGIVING

(after the Confessions have been completed)

Psalm of praise

A responsorial psalm of praise is prayed, e.g. Psalm 129 from the Fifth Sunday of Lent, Year A. Or a hymn of thanksgiving may be sung (e.g. 'Amazing Grace' or 'Holy God We Praise Thy Name'). At the end of the Act of Thanksgiving, the church lights are turned on in full.

A **Sign of Peace** is then exchanged.

Details of the Holy Week Ceremonies are announced and all who took part are thanked. The **Final Blessing** is then given.

Dismissal

Go in the peace to love and serve the Lord.
Thanks be to God.

Final Song: Instrumental music fills the church as priests and people leave.

*Rite of Penance/Gnás na hAithrí was published by Veritas Publications in 1976.

FEAST OF ST PATRICK

FOR PRESIDERS

Opening Comment

Just ten days before Easter Sunday, we keep the feast of Patrick, the patron saint of Ireland. We mark the day by praising God the creator, who sustained Patrick, and who sustains the Church, in good times and bad.

Penitential Rite: To prepare ourselves for this solemn celebration, let us call to mind our sins: (pause)
Lord Jesus, you came to reconcile us to one another and to the Father: Lord, have mercy...
Lord Jesus, you heal the wounds of sin and division: Christ, have mercy.
Lord Jesus, you intercede for us with your Father: Lord, have mercy.

Introduction to the Scripture Readings

Jeremiah 1:4-9 – Jeremiah protests that he is too young to be a prophet. Like St Patrick he is a mere 'holy youth.'
Acts 13: 46-49 – Paul speaks of the importance of bringing the Good News to gentile nations, to remote peoples like the Irish.
Luke 10:1-12, 17-20 – Describes the sending out of the 72, with power even over scorpions and snakes — a power the tradition tells us St Patrick also possessed.

The General Intercessions *(Samples)*

Introduction *(by the Presider)*
Let us bring our needs to the Lord of all nations.

Intercessions *(announced by the deacon, minister or member of the Faithful)*

1   That the people of God in Ireland may keep alive the faith that Patrick preached.
     (Pause for silent prayer)   Lord, hear us.

2.   That Christians everywhere may live in harmony and peace with each other.
     (Pause for silent prayer)   Lord, hear us.

3.   That Irish people the world over may enjoy God's favour and protection.
     (Pause for silent prayer)   Lord, hear us.

4.   That those in need, at home and abroad, may experience care and compassion.
     (Pause for silent prayer)   Lord, hear us.

5.   That our people who have died may have the light of heaven.
     (Pause for silent prayer)   Lord, hear us.

6.   That we may have divine assistance in all our needs, for which we pray quietly for a moment:
     (Long pause for silent prayer)   Lord, hear us.

Conclusion *(by the Presider)*
God of truth and beauty, you look after us through the prayer of our friends, the saints:
Keep us and all your Irish flock in your care, through Christ our Lord. Amen.

FOR LITURGY PLANNERS

Liturgical Suggestions

Best vestments are worn, white or gold, spring flowers decorate the altar (just for today) and flags are flown (Irish/European/Vatican). Penitential Rite c-iv. Gloria. Lenten gospel acclamation. Preface of Pastors. Eucharistic Prayer 3. Solemn Blessing 17 (Apostles – adapted) or 18 (All Saints).
• Presiders in Ireland are encouraged to use the Irish language during Mass: eg the Sign of the Cross, general greeting (*Go raibh an Tiarna libh/Agus leat féin*) and the introduction to the Our Father (*Le Pádraig naofa, guimís chun an Athair: Ár nAthair…*)

Songs: 'Christ Be Near At Either Hand'; 'Hail Glorious St Patrick'; 'Dóchas Linn Naomh Pádraig'.

PALM SUNDAY

FOR PRESIDERS

Opening Comment (*for Mass without Procession or Solemn Entrance*)
Today's liturgy gives us a preview of the events we will celebrate in the Easter Triduum later this week. The passion, death and resurrection of Jesus are the focus of this and every Sunday celebration.

Penitential Rite: As we prepare ourselves to celebrate these sacred mysteries, let us call to mind our sins: (pause)
You raise the dead to life in the Spirit: Lord, have mercy.
You bring pardon and peace to the sinner: Lord, have mercy.
You bring light to those in darkness: Lord, have mercy.

Introduction to the Scripture Readings
Isaiah 50:4-7 – This reading describes someone putting up with a lot of suffering. Our tradition teaches us that these lines apply to Jesus.
Philippians 2:6-11 – In this ancient hymn to Christ, we are taught that Jesus achieved glory through suffering.
Matthew 26:14 to 27:66 – This year, the Gospel of the Passion of Jesus is the version recorded by Saint Matthew. It's clear from it that Matthew believed the Jews were to blame for the death of the Messiah. However, the Church does not hold the Jewish people of today in any way responsible for Jesus' death.

The General Intercessions (*Samples*)

Introduction (*by the Presider*)
Let us bring our prayers to God, our strength, who makes haste to help us.

Intercessions (*announced by the deacon, minister or member of the Faithful*)

1. For the Church of God throughout the world,
    that all Christians may celebrate these holy days with deep faith.
    (*Pause for silent prayer*)   Lord, hear us.

2. For the Jewish people, our brothers and sisters,
    that they may continue to grow in faithfulness to the covenant.
    (*Pause for silent prayer*)   Lord, hear us.

3. For the city of Jerusalem, where many faiths meet,
    that it may be a place of forgiveness and reconciliation. (*Pause for silent prayer*) Lord, hear us.

4. For those who suffer torture and humiliation,
    that the sufferings of Christ, and his glory, may bring them hope.
    (*Pause for silent prayer*)   Lord, hear us.

5. For all those who gone before us in faith (especially N & N),
    that they may journey through the valley of death to resurrection.
    (*Pause for silent prayer*)   Lord, hear us.

Conclusion (*by the Presider*)
God of compassion, in the death and resurrection of Jesus you show your love for us:
Hear our petitions, and grant them, through Christ our Lord. Amen.

FOR LITURGY PLANNERS

Liturgical Suggestions
The Blessing of palms precedes the main Mass: texts given in Roman Missal, page 123: Penitential Rite is then omitted. (At other Masses: Penitential Rite c-v. No Gloria.)
All Masses: All stand for the Gospel (full form recommended). The homily is to be brief. Preface 19 (Palm Sunday). Eucharistic Prayer 2. Solemn Blessing 5 (The Passion of the Lord).

Songs: 'Hail Redeemer, King Divine'; 'Jesus Remember Me' (Taizé); 'Benedictus qui venit.'

The Week ahead
Monday 21 March: International Day for the Elimination of Racial Discrimination.
Thursday 24 March: Holy Thursday: also the anniversary of Archbishop Oscar Romero, shot while saying Mass on 24-3-1980.
Friday 25 March: Good Friday is a day of fast and abstinence. (The Annunciation is celebrated on 4 April this year.)
Today is Purim (Feast of Lots) in Israel, commemorating the saving of Jews living in Persia (see Book of Esther).

HOLY THURSDAY

FOR PRESIDERS

Opening Comment

The liturgy that begins now continues until we reach Easter. We are at the start of a three-day celebration of the passion, death and resurrection of Jesus. We journey from the Last Supper to Gethsemane tonight, from there to Calvary tomorrow, and from the tomb to resurrection and new life at the Vigil of Easter Sunday.

Penitential Rite: As we prepare ourselves for the celebration of the Easter Triduum, let us call to mind our sins: (pause) I confess...

Introduction to the Scripture Readings

Exodus 12:1-8, 11-14 – Contains the instructions for the celebration of the great Passover meal. In the killing of the lamb for this meal, Christian see a glimpse beforehand of the sacrifice of Jesus.

1 Corinthians 11:23-26 – Paul's account of what happened at the Last Supper is our earliest record of the event.

John 13:1-15 – In case Christians would be tempted to see the Eucharist as unrelated to everyday living, St John describes the washing of feet at the Last Supper, as a reminder that the Eucharist challenges those who partake of it to serve each other.

The General Intercessions *(Samples)*

Introduction *(by the Presider)*

In thanksgiving and praise, let us bring our petitions to God:

Intercessions *(announced by the deacon, cantor or another person)*

1.	For a spirit of service among all Christians. *(Pause for silent prayer)*	Lord, hear us.
2.	For an end to fighting and division. *(Pause for silent prayer)*	Lord, hear us.
3.	For the poor, the hungry, the lonely. *(Pause for silent prayer)*	Lord, hear us.
4.	For carers and all who comfort the sick. *(Pause for silent prayer)*	Lord, hear us.
5.	For people in need of healing. *(Pause for silent prayer)*	Lord, hear us.
6.	For our dead (especially N & N). *(Pause for silent prayer)*	Lord, hear us.
7.	For our own needs, which we remember now in silence... *(Long pause for silent prayer)*	Lord, hear us.

Conclusion *(by the Presider)*

God our creator, we praise and thank you for your goodness:
Help us in our needs and hear our prayers, through Jesus Christ our Lord. Amen.

FOR LITURGY PLANNERS

Liturgical Suggestions

Penitential Rite a. Gloria is included (bells) but no Alleluia. Washing of feet follows Gospel/homily, then Intercessions (no Creed). Presentation of the gifts may include *Trócaire* boxes or other gifts for the poor. Preface of the Holy Eucharist 1. Eucharistic Prayer 1 (with three special insertions.) Include the Sign of Peace. No blessing today – procession to Place of Repose follows Prayer after Communion. (Announce the times of the Triduum liturgies before the Prayer.)

Songs: 'Love is his Word'; 'The Lord's my Shepherd'; 'One Bread, One Body'; 'Ag Críost an Síol'.
Washing of Feet: 'The Lord Jesus...'; 'Ubi Caritas' *(Taizé)*
Procession to Place of Repose: 'Pange Lingua/Tantum Ergo'; 'Céad Míle Fáilte Romhat'; 'O Sacrament Most Holy'.
At Place of Repose: 'Stay Here and Keep Watch' *(Taizé)*.

Good Friday songs: *Stations of the Cross: 'Were you there...?'; 'At the cross her station keeping'.*
Celebration of the Passion: 'The Reproaches', 'God of Mercy and Compassion'; 'Praise to the Holiest'.

THE EASTER VIGIL

FOR PRESIDERS

Opening Comment (*after the Service of Light and Exsultet*)
We gather around the Easter candle, celebrating the Lord's resurrection. With that light to illumine our way, we remember how God has cared for humanity from the dawn of time. These readings remind us what happened at the highpoints of our history.

Introduction to the Scripture Readings
Three Old Testament readings are chosen from these seven:
Genesis 1:1 to 2:2 The first chapter of the first book of the Bible gives the story of creation, the foundation of God's care for all the world. This love for humanity was seen even more clearly in the death and resurrection of Jesus, which made us into a new creation through the mystery we celebrate this night.
Genesis 22:1-8 The heartbreaking story of Abraham offering up his only child Isaac teaches that true sacrifice is about faith and obedience rather than slaughter. The promise that Abraham would be the father of many nations was fulfilled when Jesus died and rose to life. All people can now share the new life by being baptised into God's chosen people.
Exodus 14 to 15:1 (not optional). God led his people from slavery to freedom through the Red Sea waters. Through the waters of baptism, God forms a new family of Christian people, set free from the slavery of sin.
Isaiah 54:5-14 The love of God is everlasting, as sure as the love of husband and wife. Even if the mountains should fall, God's love for all people will never fail. They will be as beautiful as the New Jerusalem, a city built of priceless jewels.
Isaiah 55:1-11 All are welcome to come to the water and be baptised: salvation is freely offered to every member of humanity.
Baruch 3:9-15, 32 to 4:4 God's people are invited to return to the fountain of wisdom, where they can find knowledge, strength and understanding. The cleansing water of baptism is a new vision of this fountain, which brings all people to salvation.
Ezekiel 36:16-28 Through the waters of baptism, men and women discover a new heart and a new spirit. The heart of stone, cold from selfishness, is removed and a heart of flesh, full of warm compassion, is given in its place.

New Testament readings
Romans 6:3-11 Baptism is a way of dying with Christ. Entering the waters of baptism, people go into the tomb. But then, with Christ, they rise. The victory over death we celebrate this night is the victory of all the baptised.
Matthew: 28:1-10 The angel tells the women that Jesus is risen: then they meet him and hear his message, not to be afraid.

The General Intercessions (*after the Liturgy of Baptism*)

> **Introduction** (*by the Presider*)
> My friends, God's love has no end: let us bring our prayers to the Lord:

> **Intercessions** (*announced by the deacon, cantor or another person*)
> *Samples for Easter Sunday can be used (see following page)*

> **Conclusion** (*by the Presider*)
> God of life and power, your love supports your people all through life and beyond:
> Hear the prayers we make this holy night, through Jesus Christ, our risen Lord. Amen.

FOR LITURGY PLANNERS

Liturgical Suggestions
Preface of Easter 1 ('On this Easter Night'). Eucharistic Prayer 3. Solemn Blessing 6 (Easter Vigil). Dismissal with multiple alleluias.

Songs: 'The Light of Christ'; 'Ag Críost an Síol'; 'Christ is Alive'.

EASTER SUNDAY

FOR PRESIDERS

Opening Comment

This Easter morning we celebrate the central mystery of our faith, the resurrection of Jesus Christ from the dead. He suffered on the cross and died for us, but now he is risen!

Introductory Rites: Filled with the spirit of Easter joy, let us proclaim the might and glory of God, as we sing (say): Glory to God in the highest...

Introduction to the Scripture Readings

Acts 10:34, 37-43 – Peter sums up the whole Paschal Mystery – the passion, death and resurrection of Jesus.
Colossians 3:1-4 – We too can share the glory of Christ.
Or 1 Corinthians 5:6-8 – We should celebrate Easter by putting aside any trace of wickedness in us.
John 20:1-9 – In John's description of the resurrection, Mary Magdalene is the first to see the empty tomb.

The General Intercessions *(Samples)*

Introduction *(by the Presider)*
We bring our prayers to God, whose love for us has no end.

Intercessions *(announced by the deacon, cantor or another person)*

1. That those becoming Christian through baptism this Easter time
    may imitate the faith of those already baptised. *(Pause for silent prayer)*   Lord, hear us.

2. That all the nations of the earth, particularly peoples at war,
    may learn to walk the path of reconciliation and justice. *(Pause for silent prayer)*   Lord, hear us.

3. That the hopeless and the lost
    may find direction and courage through the power of Jesus, our Risen Saviour.
    (Pause for silent prayer)   Lord, hear us.

4. That the people in our community who suffer illness or anxiety
    may experience healing and peace. *(Pause for silent prayer)*   Lord, hear us.

5. That those who have died recently may share the glory of Christ's resurrection
    (especially N & N) and that all from this community who have died since
    last Easter may find rest: (we remember them now...) *(Pause for silent prayer)*   Lord, hear us.

Conclusion *(by the Presider)*
O God, you lead your people from defeat to triumph:
Hear and grant our prayers, through Christ our Lord. Amen.

FOR LITURGY PLANNERS

Liturgical Suggestions

Alternative Opening Prayer. The Sequence may be read or sung after the Second Reading. The Alleluia follows it: this is sung at every Mass today. The Creed is usually replaced with the renewal of baptismal promises, following the format given in the Missal with the Easter Sunday Mass prayers. After this, the people are sprinkled with Easter water. (This is why the penitential Rite is omitted and the Gloria follows the opening greeting.) Preface of Easter 1. Eucharistic Prayer 1 (special form of *In union with the whole Church* and *Father accept this offering*). Solemn Blessing 6 (Easter Sunday). Dismissal with multiple alleluias.

Songs: 'Jesus Christ is Risen Today'; 'A New Hymn of Praise'; 'This is the Day'.

The Week Ahead

Monday 28 March: Easter Monday (Bank Holiday).
Wednesday 30 March: Doctor's Day (USA).
Friday 1 April: April Fool's Day (First Friday).
Saturday 2 April: International Children's Book Day (UN).

SECOND SUNDAY OF EASTER

FOR PRESIDERS

Opening Comment

Even though a week has passed since Easter Sunday, today's liturgy is still filled with good news. We praise God for the life and love poured out for us in the raising of Jesus, which makes divine mercy possible, and available to all.

Penitential Rite: *Let us celebrate this mercy: God's love for us never ends! (pause)*

Lord Jesus, you raise us to new life: Lord, have mercy.

Lord Jesus, you forgive us our sins: Christ, have mercy.

Lord Jesus, you feed us with your body and blood: Lord, have mercy.

Introduction to the Scripture Readings

Acts 2:42-47 – For the whole season of Easter, the first reading comes from the Acts of the Apostles; today's segment describes how the early Christians lived.

1 Peter 1:3-9 – In the second reading, Peter sets out the reasons for our hope.

John 20:19-31 – The Gospel contains the story of Thomas coming to terms with Jesus' resurrection.

The General Intercessions *(Samples)*

Introduction *(by the Presider)*

Let us bring our prayers to God, whose love for us has no end.

Intercessions *(announced by the deacon, cantor or another person)*

1. For those who have been baptised this Easter and for every one of us already baptised,
    that the faith of all may grow stronger each day. *(Pause for silent prayer)*   Lord, hear us.

2. For people who struggle with doubt,
    that they may become convinced of Christ's victory over sin and death.
    (Pause for silent prayer)   Lord, hear us.

3. For our community,
    that we may grow in love and care for each other. *(Pause for silent prayer)*   Lord, hear us.

4. For the sick, and those facing operations,
    that they may experience healing and new strength. *(Pause for silent prayer)*   Lord, hear us.

5. For those who have died (especially N & N),
    that they may share the glory of Christ's resurrection. *(Pause for silent prayer)* Lord, hear us.

Conclusion *(by the Presider)*

Loving God, you are our help, our strength and our salvation:

Hear and answer the prayers we make in faith, through Christ our Lord. Amen.

FOR LITURGY PLANNERS

Liturgical Suggestions

The Easter Water may be sprinkled at the end of the Penitential Rite c-vi. Alleluia is sung at every Mass. Preface of Easter 1. Eucharistic Prayer 3. Solemn Blessing 6 (Easter Sunday). Dismissal with alleluias. The Second Sunday of Easter is also Divine Mercy Sunday. The image of 'The Divine Mercy' may be displayed in the church, and attention drawn to it at the start of Mass.

Songs: 'Christ is Alive'; 'Now the Green Blade Rises'; 'Ag Críost an Síol'.

The Week Ahead

Monday 4 April: The Annunciation is celebrated (transferred from Good Friday).

Thursday 7 April: National Mourning Day in Rwanda (Genocide Remembrance Day). World Health Day (UN).

Saturday 9 April: 'Day of Valour' is marked in the Philippines (Bataan Day).

THIRD SUNDAY OF EASTER

FOR PRESIDERS

Opening Comment

During the Easter season the Church continues to celebrate Jesus' resurrection from the dead. Today, we join together to worship God, who has brought about this great victory over sin and death.

Penitential Rite: In joy and gratitude, we praise God who saves us (pause)

You raise the dead to life in the Spirit: Lord, have mercy.

You bring pardon and peace to the sinner: Christ, have mercy.

You bring light to those in darkness: Lord, have mercy.

Introduction to the Scripture Readings

Acts 3:13-15, 17-19 – Many of St Peter's words are found in the first two readings. The first contains his speech on Pentecost day, and the second is part of one of his letters.

1 Peter 1:17-21 – Peter reminds us that Christ paid the price of our salvation.

Luke 24:13-35 – The Gospel describes the appearance of Jesus to the two disciples on the road to Emmaus.

The General Intercessions *(Samples)*

Introduction *(by the Presider)*

Because the Lord is our refuge and strength, let us bring forward our prayers.

Intercessions *(announced by the deacon, cantor or another person)*

1. For all Christians,
    that they may accept the scriptures and live by God's word.
    (Pause for silent prayer)   Lord, hear us.

2. For those who haven't yet heard the Good News,
    that the lives of believers may bring light and hope to all in darkness.
    (Pause for silent prayer)   Lord, hear us.

3. For people who travel, like the two on the road to Emmaus,
    that they may recognise Christ walking with them. *(Pause for silent prayer)*   Lord, hear us.

4. For those who suffer in mind and body, at home and abroad,
    that they may experience peace within. *(Pause for silent prayer)*   Lord, hear us.

5. For all who have gone before us in faith (especially N & N),
    that they may know happiness forever at God's right hand. *(Pause for silent prayer)* Lord, hear us.

Conclusion *(by the Presider)*

Lord our God, you show us the path of life:

Support us by your presence and help us every step of the way, through Christ our Lord. Amen.

FOR LITURGY PLANNERS

Liturgical Suggestions

Penitential Rite c-v. Or the Rite may be replaced with the Blessing and Sprinkling of Holy Water. (See Roman Missal page 387 – use formula c, for the Easter Season. The Gloria follows the sprinkling.) Preface of Easter 5. Eucharistic Prayer 2. Solemn Blessing 7 (Easter Season).

Songs: 'Bring, all you Dear-Bought Nations'; 'Christ Be Our Light'; 'He is Lord'.

The Week Ahead

Tuesday 12 April: Cosmonauts' Day in Russia.

Wednesday 13: St Martin I, who died in 655, was the last pope to be venerated as a martyr.

Saturday 16 April: Queen Margrethe's birthday is celebrated in Denmark and Greenland.

FOURTH SUNDAY OF EASTER

FOR PRESIDERS

Opening Comment

The fourth Sunday of Easter is often called Good Shepherd Sunday, because the readings are about the care we receive from Christ, our true shepherd. Today is also the day of prayer for vocations.

Penitential Rite: Knowing that God cares for us every step of the way, we rely on divine forgiveness:

Lord Jesus, you have shown us the way to the Father: Lord, have mercy.

Lord Jesus, you have given us the consolation of the truth: Christ, have mercy.

Lord Jesus, you are the Good Shepherd, leading us into everlasting life: Lord, have mercy.

Introduction to the Scripture Readings

Acts 2:14, 36-41 – Just like last week, St Peter's words are found in the first two readings. The first contains another part of his speech on Pentecost day, and the second is again part of one of his letters.

1 Peter 2:20-25 – Here Peter calls Christ the shepherd and guardian of our souls.

John 10:1-10 – Jesus describes himself as the gate of the sheepfold, who comes so that we might have life to the full.

The General Intercessions *(Samples)*

Introduction *(by the Presider)*
Confident that God's care is boundless, let us bring forward our prayers.

Intercessions *(announced by the deacon, cantor or another person)*

1. For the pastors of the Church,
   that they may imitate Christ, the Good Shepherd. *(Pause for silent prayer)*   Lord, hear us.

2. For young people,
   that they may be open to the call to serve God's people. *(Pause for silent prayer)*   Lord, hear us.

3. For members of the caring professions,
   that the gentle love of Christ may inspire them. *(Pause for silent prayer)*   Lord, hear us.

4. For those who work on the land,
   that their labour may bear fruit in a rich harvest. *(Pause for silent prayer)*   Lord, hear us.

5. For all who have died in Christ (especially N & N),
   that they may dwell in God's house forever. *(Pause for silent prayer)*   Lord, hear us.

Conclusion *(by the Presider)*
Loving God, like a caring shepherd you bring us along the right path:
Hear our prayers and grant us your help, through Christ our Lord. Amen.

FOR LITURGY PLANNERS

Liturgical Suggestions

Today is the Day of Prayer for Vocations. Penitential Rite c-vii. Preface of Easter 2. Eucharistic Prayer 3. Solemn Blessing 7 (Easter Season).

Songs: 'The Lord's My Shepherd'; 'My Soul is Longing for your Peace'; 'Shepherd me O God'.

The Week Ahead

Thursday 21 April: Mawlid an Nabi (Islam) commemorates the birthday of the Prophet Muhammad.
Friday 22 April: Earth Day.
Saturday 23 April: St George's Day (Patron Saint of England).

FIFTH SUNDAY OF EASTER

FOR PRESIDERS

Opening Comment
Today's liturgy puts the life-giving words of Jesus before us. He is the Way, the Truth and the Life, the one in whom we can place all our trust. Because we believe these things, we gather to praise God.

Penitential Rite: Trusting in divine forgiveness, let us call to mind our sins: (pause)
Lord Jesus, you raise us to new life: Lord, have mercy.
Lord Jesus, you forgive us our sins: Christ, have mercy.
Lord Jesus, you feed us with your body and blood: Lord, have mercy.

Introduction to the Scripture Readings
Acts 6:1-7 – This describes the selection of the first deacons, a response to a pressing need in the early Church.
1 Peter 2:4-9 – Peter writes about our calling as Christians.
John 14:1-12 – Jesus describes himself as our saviour, the one who prepares a place for us.

The General Intercessions *(Samples)*

Introduction *(by the Presider)*
The Lord looks on those who revere him, so let us make our prayers known to him.

Intercessions *(announced by the deacon, cantor or another person)*

1. For those who serve the Church as deacons,
    that they may be good servants of God's people. *(Pause for silent prayer)*   Lord, hear us.

2. For all who serve humanity in the caring professions,
    that they may be concerned for the spirit as well as the body.
    (Pause for silent prayer)   Lord, hear us.

3. For people at risk: widows, orphans, the homeless, the poor,
    that the Christian community may always see to their care.
    (Pause for silent prayer)   Lord, hear us.

4. For those who are anxious in the face of suffering and death,
    that the Lord's words may console them. *(Pause for silent prayer)*   Lord, hear us.

5. For all who have left this world, in the hope of rising again *(especially N & N)*,
    that they may be where Christ is, eternally. *(Pause for silent prayer)*   Lord, hear us.

Conclusion *(by the Presider)*
Father in heaven, we place all our hope in you, as we entrust these prayers to your love, confident that you will grant them, through Christ our Lord. Amen.

FOR LITURGY PLANNERS

Liturgical Suggestions
Penitential Rite c-vi. Or replace with the blessing and sprinkling of holy water (given at the start of Mass in the Roman Missal; use prayer c – Easter Season. The Gloria follows the sprinkling.) Preface of Easter 3. Eucharistic Prayer 1. Solemn Blessing 7 (Easter Season).

Songs: 'Be Not Afraid'; 'May Your Love Be Upon Us, O Lord'; 'Take and Eat'.

The Week Ahead
Monday 25 April: St Mark is honoured, especially in Venice. ANZAC Day in Australia and New Zealand.
Wednesday 27 April: Administrative Professionals' Day in the USA (formerly Secretaries' Day).
Thursday 28 April: Day of Mourning for Persons Killed or Injured in the Workplace (Canada).
Friday 29 April: Good Friday (Julian Calendar). Next Sunday is the Orthodox Easter, or 'Pascha'.

SIXTH SUNDAY OF EASTER

FOR PRESIDERS

Opening Comment

Each Sunday in Easter time, we celebrate the gifts we have received in Baptism and Confirmation. We rejoice that the Spirit is our Advocate, who continues to support us in the difficulties of life.

Penitential Rite: As we gather for this celebration, we rely on the Spirit's help in our weakness: (pause)
You raise the dead to life in the Spirit: Lord, have mercy.
You bring pardon and peace to the sinner: Christ, have mercy.
You bring light to those in darkness: Lord, have mercy.

Introduction to the Scripture Readings

Acts 8:5-8, 14-17 – Describes the continuing successes in the early Church, and the giving of the Spirit to new believers.
1 Peter 3:15-18 – Peter writes that Christians should be able to give a reason for the hope that is in them.
John 14:15-21 – Jesus repeats his commandment of love, and promises the gift of the Spirit.

The General Intercessions *(Samples)*

Introduction *(by the Presider)*
The works of God are tremendous, so with confidence we make our prayers known.

Intercessions *(announced by the deacon, cantor or another person)*

1. For those who are celebrating the Sacrament of Confirmation this year,
    that the Spirit may be their guide throughout life. *(Pause for silent prayer)*   Lord, hear us.

2. For all the people of God,
    that the Spirit may help them explain their faith to people who are searching.
    (Pause for silent prayer)   Lord, hear us.

3. For those who are crippled or paralysed,
    that the Spirit of power and strength may help them each day.
    (Pause for silent prayer)   Lord, hear us.

4. For young people preparing for exams,
    that the Spirit may remind them of all they have learned. *(Pause for silent prayer)* Lord, hear us.

5. For our brothers and sisters who have died (especially N & N),
    that they may be raised to life in the Spirit. *(Pause for silent prayer)*   Lord, hear us.

6. For this community and all our own needs,
    (which we remember in silence – *long pause for silent prayer)*
    that God's Spirit may always sustain us.   Lord, hear us.

Conclusion *(by the Presider)*
God of love and compassion, you never reject our prayer:
Let your good Spirit guide us each day, through Christ our Lord. Amen.

FOR LITURGY PLANNERS

Liturgical Suggestions

Penitential Rite c-v. First Opening Prayer. Preface of Easter 4. Eucharistic Prayer 2. Solemn Blessing 7 (Easter Season).

Songs: 'Christ Be Beside Me'; Spirit of the Living God'; 'Ubi Caritas (Taizé)'.

The Week Ahead

Monday 2 May: Bank holiday. Our Lady of Czestochowa is celebrated in Poland.
Tuesday 3 May: Saints Philip and James, apostles. World Press Freedom Day (UN).
Thursday 5 May: 'Ascension Thursday'. Battle of Puebla Day is celebrated in Mexico (Cinco de Mayo).
Friday 6 May: Pentecost Novena begins today (First Friday).

ASCENSION OF THE LORD

FOR PRESIDERS

Opening Comment

We celebrate the Ascension of Jesus today. We remember his sending out of the disciples, and his promise to remain with us until the end of time.

Penitential Rite: Assured by Christ's words, we renew our trust in his continuing help: (pause)
Lord Jesus, you raise us to new life: Lord, have mercy.
Lord Jesus, you forgive us our sins: Christ, have mercy.
Lord Jesus, you feed us with your body and blood: Lord, have mercy.

Introduction to the Scripture Readings

Acts 1:1-11 – Luke describes the Ascension: this excerpt is taken from the very beginning of the book of Acts.
Ephesians 1:17-23 – Paul interprets the event as Christ's exaltation at the right hand of the Father.
Matthew 28:16-20 – Matthew's description of the command to make disciples of all nations, given at the Ascension.

The General Intercessions *(Samples)*

Introduction *(by the Presider)*
With confidence, we bring our prayers before God, the Most High.

Intercessions *(announced by the deacon, cantor or another person)*

1.   For Christian missionaries all over the world,
     that God's Spirit may fill them with fresh enthusiasm. *(Pause for silent prayer)*   Lord, hear us.

2.   For all of us on our journey of faith,
     that Christ's presence may sustain us, all our days. *(Pause for silent prayer)*   Lord, hear us.

3.   For those who work in the world of communications,
     that their efforts may serve humankind. *(Pause for silent prayer)*   Lord, hear us.

4.   For absent friends, and all those we have lost contact with,
     that God's Spirit may heal broken relationships. *(Pause for silent prayer)*   Lord, hear us.

5.   For those whose life in this world has ended *(especially N & N)*,
     that where Christ has gone, they may soon follow. *(Pause for silent prayer)*   Lord, hear us.

6.   A moment's quiet prayer for all our own particular needs…
     (Long pause for silent prayer)   Lord, hear us.

Conclusion *(by the Presider)*
God most high, king of all the earth, you care for all you have made:
Hear these prayers we make in faith, through Christ our Lord. Amen.

FOR LITURGY PLANNERS

Liturgical Suggestions

Today is World Communications Day – a day to highlight and encourage the work of those involved in the communications ministries of the parish (e.g. parish newsletter, website, etc.). Penitential Rite c-vi. Alternative Opening Prayer. Preface of the Ascension 1. Eucharistic Prayer 3. Solemn Blessing 8 (Ascension).

Songs: 'Let The Earth Rejoice And Sing'; 'Now the Green Blade Rises'; 'Praise to the Holiest'.

The Week Ahead

Tuesday 10 May: Father Damien, now Blessed Damien of Moloka'i.
Thursday 12 May: International Nurses/Midwives Day (UN).
Friday 13 May: Our Lady of Fatima is celebrated.
Saturday 14 May: St Matthias, apostle. Independence Day in Israel.

PENTECOST SUNDAY

FOR PRESIDERS

Opening Comment *(Mass During the Day)*
Today we celebrate 'the great beginning of the Church,' the day the Holy Spirit first came to confused and frightened disciples. We praise God for this great Gift, and ask for a new outpouring in our day.
   Penitential Rite: As we prepare ourselves to enter into this great celebration,
   let us call to mind our need of the Spirit's help in our weakness...
   You raise the dead to life in the Spirit: Lord, have mercy.
   You bring pardon and peace to the sinner: Christ, have mercy.
   You bring light to those in darkness: Lord, have mercy.

Introduction to the Scripture Readings *(Mass During the Day)*
Acts 2:1-11 – The events of the first Pentecost are described vividly.
1 Corinthians 12:3-7, 12-13 – The Spirit binds all the members of the Body of Christ into one.
John 20:19-23 – The promise of the Holy Spirit is given in today's Gospel.

The General Intercessions *(Samples)*

   Introduction *(by the Presider)*
   Conscious of the Spirit praying within us, let us present our petitions with confidence.

   Intercessions *(announced by the deacon, cantor or another person)*
   1.   That the Spirit may fill the leaders of the Church
         and put new life into all the bishops. *(Pause for silent prayer)*   Lord, hear us.

   2.   That the Spirit may invigorate all the members of the Church
         and help those baptised and confirmed this year to grow in grace.
         (Pause for silent prayer)   Lord, hear us.

   3.   That the Spirit may give fresh enthusiasm to all who minister in this community
         and swell the numbers of those who serve the Lord here. *(Pause for silent prayer)* Lord, hear us.

   4.   That the Spirit may renew the face of the earth
         and bring peace to the world and healing to those who suffer.
         (Pause for silent prayer)   Lord, hear us.

   5.   That the Spirit may bring life to those who have died (especially N & N),
         and lead all the faithful departed home to heaven. *(Pause for silent prayer)*   Lord, hear us.

   Conclusion *(by the Presider)*
   God our creator, your Spirit brings us to life and sustains us:
   Hear the prayers we are inspired to make, through Christ our Lord. Amen.

FOR LITURGY PLANNERS

Liturgical Suggestions
Mass During the Day: Penitential Rite c-v. Opening Prayer on page 282 (Roman Missal). The Sequence is prayed, perhaps by many readers, or it may be sung. Preface of Pentecost. Eucharistic Prayer 1 (special form of *In union with the whole Church*). Solemn Blessing 9 (The Holy Spirit). Dismissal with muptiple alleluias.
Vigil Mass: Mass prayers in Roman Missal, pages 280 to 281. Readings in Lectionary Volume I, pages 596 to 600.
* *The Easter season ends today. The Paschal Candle is moved from its Easter place by the ambo, to the font.*

Songs: 'Veni Creator Spiritus'; 'Come O Creator Spirit Blest'; Veni Sancte Spiritus *(Taizé)*'; 'Send Forth Your Spirit O Lord'.

The Week Ahead
Friday 20 May: St Bernardine of Siena, patron of advertisers, communications and public relations personnel.
Saturday 21 May: St Christopher Magallánes and companions (executed in Mexico in 1927).

TRINITY SUNDAY

FOR PRESIDERS

Opening Comment

We are invited to reflect on the mystery of God on this Trinity Sunday, as we gather to worship the One who creates, redeems and sanctifies, three persons, one God, without end.

Penitential Rite: To prepare ourselves for this celebration, let us call to mind our sins:
I confess...

Introduction to the Scripture Readings

Exodus 34:4-6, 8-9 – God is described in terms of tenderness and compassion, kindness and faithfulness.
2 Corinthians 13:11-13 – A plea by Paul for unity in the Church, in the grace of Jesus, the love of God and the fellowship of the Holy Spirit.
John 3:16-18 – Jesus came to show God's love for the world: no one who believes will be condemned.

The General Intercessions *(Samples)*

Introduction *(by the Presider)*
Let us give glory to the great God, presenting our needs with trust and confidence.

Intercessions *(announced by the deacon, cantor or another person)*

1. For all believers,
    that they may know and experience the love of God. *(Pause for silent prayer)*   Lord, hear us.

2. For people who search for the truth,
    that God may embrace them with love and draw them to faith.
    (Pause for silent prayer)   Lord, hear us.

3. For all who seek peace and justice,
    that they may inspire the peoples of the earth to work together.
    (Pause for silent prayer)   Lord, hear us.

4. For this community, for all who worship in this place,
    that our Christian faith may be visible in the kind way we treat each other.
    (Pause for silent prayer)   Lord, hear us.

5. For those we have lost to death (especially N & N),
    that they may give glory and praise to God for ever more.
    (Pause for silent prayer)   Lord, hear us.

6. For our own needs, which we remember now... *(long pause for silent prayer)*   Lord, hear us.

Conclusion *(by the Presider)*
God of infinite mercy, hear the prayers of your people
– who give praise for all the good things that come from you, through Christ our Lord. Amen.

FOR LITURGY PLANNERS

Liturgical Suggestions

Penitential Rite a. Alternative Opening Prayer. Preface of the Holy Trinity. Eucharistic Prayer 3. Solemn Blessing 11 (Ordinary Time 2).

Songs: 'All people that on earth do dwell'; 'Immortal, Invisible, God only Wise'; 'Holy God We Praise Thy Name'.

The Week Ahead

Monday 23 May: Vesak or Visakah Puja ('Buddha Day') is celebrated in Buddhism.
Wednesday 25 May: Africa Day.
Thursday 26 May: 'Corpus Christi'.

THE BODY AND BLOOD OF CHRIST
(CORPUS CHRISTI)

FOR PRESIDERS

Opening Comment

Today's liturgy invites us to reflect on God's care for the family of faith, especially through the gift of divine nourishment on our pilgrimage through life.

Penitential Rite: As we enter into this celebration, let us praise God who sustains us all our days: (pause)

Lord Jesus, you raise us to new life: Lord, have mercy.

Lord Jesus, you forgive us our sins: Christ, have mercy.

Lord Jesus, you feed us with your body and blood: Lord, have mercy.

Introduction to the Scripture Readings

Deuteronomy 8:2-3, 14-16 – Contains Moses' reminder of how God sustained his people in the desert with the gift of manna.

1 Corinthians 10:16-17 – Paul reminds us that in sharing the bread of life at Mass, we become one body.

John 6:51-58 – In the Gospel Jesus says he himself is the living bread for believers.

The General Intercessions *(Samples)*

Introduction *(by the Presider)*

Let us bring our prayers before the Lord, whose sons and daughters are blessed.

Intercessions *(announced by the deacon, cantor or another person)*

1. For all who hold the Catholic faith,
    that their belief in the presence of Christ may grow stronger each time they receive the Eucharist.
    (Pause for silent prayer)   Lord, hear us.

2. For those who rarely join in the Mass,
    that the loving embrace of the Father may draw them into the community of faith.
    (Pause for silent prayer)   Lord, hear us.

3. For all who are hungry in a world of plenty,
    that those who worship the God of compassion may continue to share with those in need.
    (Pause for silent prayer)   Lord, hear us.

4. For people who suffer, in mind, body or spirit,
    that the Bread of Life they receive may bring them comfort and peace.
    (Pause for silent prayer)   Lord, hear us.

5. For those have gone before us in faith (especially N & N),
    that they may be raised up at the last day. *(Pause for silent prayer)*   Lord, hear us.

Conclusion *(by the Presider)*

God of infinite generosity, you sent your Son to share our burdens and our hopes, to be our life and strength: Hear the prayers we make in his name, who lives and reigns with you, forever and ever. Amen.

FOR LITURGY PLANNERS

Liturgical Suggestions

Communion under both species is often given today. It's also a suitable day for First Communion and for commissioning Ministers of the Eucharist. If ministers usually bring Communion to the Sick, send them out solemnly from Mass today with words like these: *'May the Lord bless you N, as you bring the body and blood of Christ to our brothers and sisters who are sick. Tell them they are in our prayers: ask them to remember us before God.'* Penitential Rite c-vi. Alternative Opening Prayer. Shorter form of Sequence (last three verses) may be prayed by many voices or sung. Preface of the Holy Eucharist 2. Eucharistic Prayer 2. Solemn Blessing 13 (Ordinary Time 4).

Songs: 'One Bread, One Body'; 'See Us Lord About Thine Altar'; 'I am the Bread of Life'.

The Week Ahead

Monday 30 May: Bank holiday in Northern Ireland and Britain. Memorial Day in the USA. Canary Islands Day in Spain.

Tues 31 May: Visitation of Our Lady to Elizabeth.

Friday 3 June: The Sacred Heart of Jesus (First Friday). Anniversary of the death of Blessed John XXIII in 1963.

CEMETERY SUNDAY

FOR PRESIDERS

Opening Comment

We gather on this summer Sunday to pray for the dead buried around us here and for all the dead. We pray with confidence that God will raise his much-loved sons and daughters to new life.

Penitential Rite: To prepare ourselves for this celebration, let us call to mind our sins – and God's forgiveness: (pause)

You raise the dead to life in the Spirit: Lord, have mercy.

You bring pardon and peace to the sinner: Christ, have mercy.

You bring light to those in darkness: Lord, have mercy.

Introduction to the Scripture Readings

Lamentations 3:17-26 – People are heartbroken in the face of death, but those who hope in God will not be disappointed.

1 Corinthians 15:51-57 – Death is all around us in a cemetery, but even here, we can rejoice in Christ's victory over death.

Luke 23:44-46, 50, 52-53, 24:1-6 – The body of Jesus was also laid in a tomb, but he rose again. All our dead will too.

The General Intercessions *(Samples)*

Introduction *(by the Presider)*

My brothers and sisters, those who hope in God will not be disappointed.

Trusting in God's promises, let us bring our prayers forward.

Intercessions *(announced by the deacon, cantor or another person)*

1. For our relatives and friends who have died,
   that they may rest from their labours, since their good deeds go with them.
   (Pause for silent prayer)   Lord, hear us.

2. For all who have been buried in this cemetery since it first opened,
   that they may rise and sing the glory of God on the last day.
   (Pause for silent prayer)   Lord, hear us.

3. For those who mourn because the one they love has died,
   that God's comforting arms may embrace them and bring them peace.
   (Pause for silent prayer)   Lord, hear us.

4. For all of us who gather here to pray,
   that we may be reunited in paradise when all grief and sadness is behind us.
   (Pause for silent prayer)   Lord, hear us.

5. A moment's quiet prayer for all our needs of today...
   (Long pause for silent prayer)   Lord, hear us.

Conclusion *(by the Presider)*

God, our hope and light, look on your people who pray for their dead:

Grant our prayers for their salvation, through Jesus Christ our Lord. Amen.

FOR LITURGY PLANNERS

Liturgical Suggestions

Prepare a list beforehand of those buried in the cemetery in the past year; read this out at the start, or during the General Intercessions. Consider replacing the penitential rite with the blessing and sprinkling of Holy Water; graves may also be blessed at this part of Mass (involve several people in these blessings). Mass prayers in Roman Missal (See also the Order of Christian Funerals 1991, pages 216 to 218.) Old Testament reading is in Lectionary Volume III, page 854, followed by psalm, page 855; epistle, page 867; Gospel, page 878. Preface of Christian Death 4 or 5. Eucharistic Prayer 2. Include the Sign of Peace.

Songs: 'Abide with Me'; 'Be not Afraid'; 'The Lord's My Shepherd'; 'I am the Bread of Life'; 'He is Lord'.

TENTH SUNDAY IN ORDINARY TIME

FOR PRESIDERS

Opening Comment

Now that Easter and all the feasts that follow it have been celebrated, the journey through the Sundays of the year starts again. From now until next Advent, we will listen to St Matthew's Gospel each Sunday, and discover Jesus through the eyes of Matthew, the tax collector who was chosen to be one of the Twelve.

Penitential Rite: To prepare ourselves to listen to God's word and share the bread of life, let us call to mind our sins: (pause)
I confess...

Introduction to the Scripture Readings

Hosea 6:3-6 – God's love for all people is certain, but people who love God experience this best.
Romans 4:18-25 – Between now and mid-September, the second reading each Sunday is from Romans, one of Paul's greatest letters. Today's section reflects on Abraham's faith. Our faith can have the same effect as his, if we believe in Jesus.
Matthew 9:9-13 – The call of Matthew, the author of this Gospel, is described in today's excerpt: Jesus explains that it's not always the most worthy who are chosen!

The General Intercessions *(Samples)*

Introduction *(by the Presider)*
Sisters and brothers, let us pray to the Lord who supports us in days of distress.

Intercessions *(announced by the deacon, cantor or another person)*

1. For the Church,
   that it may be a sign of the mercy and compassion of Jesus.
   (Pause for silent prayer)   Lord, hear us.

2. For people on the fringes of society,
   that they may hear the message that salvation is for all. *(Pause for silent prayer)* Lord, hear us.

3. For Christians, Jews and Muslims, all children of Abraham,
   that they may grow in mutual love and respect. *(Pause for silent prayer)*   Lord, hear us.

4. For those preparing for exams these June days,
   that the prayers of the community may support them. *(Pause for silent prayer)* Lord, hear us.

5. For our people who have died (especially N & N),
   that they may be raised to life, as Christ was raised. *(Pause for silent prayer)*   Lord, hear us.

Conclusion *(by the Presider)*
God of gods, you support your people when they call to you:
Be with us in days of happiness and of distress, and grant our prayers, through Christ our Lord. Amen.

FOR LITURGY PLANNERS

Liturgical Suggestions

Penitential Rite b. First Opening Prayer. Preface for Sundays in Ordinary Time 4. Eucharistic Prayer 1 (which honours Abraham, the focus of the Second reading). Solemn Blessing 10 (Ordinary Time 1).

Songs: 'Here I am, Lord'; 'Come To Me'; 'Let us Build the City of God'.

The Week Ahead

Monday 6 June: June Bank Holiday. Jerusalem Day (Yom Yerushalayim) is celebrated in Israel.
Thursday 9 June: St Colmcille (or Columba), secondary patron of Ireland.
Friday 10 June: National Day in Portugal.

ELEVENTH SUNDAY IN ORDINARY TIME

FOR PRESIDERS

Opening Comment
As people loved and chosen by God, we gather to listen and share, before being sent out to live what we believe.

Penitential Rite: The Gospel challenges our faith, so we turn to our God of healing and mercy: (pause)
Lord Jesus, you healed the sick: Lord, have mercy.
Lord Jesus, you forgave sinners: Christ, have mercy.
Lord Jesus, you gave us yourself to heal us and bring us strength: Lord, have mercy.

Introduction to the Scripture Readings
Exodus 19:2-6 – The first reading contains a reminder of God's care for the people of Israel, our ancestors in faith.
Romans 5:6-11 – St Paul explains that the death of Jesus proves God's love.
Matthew 9:36 to 10:8 – In the Gospel, Jesus shows compassion for the people by appointing apostles to heal the sick and cast out demons.

The General Intercessions *(Samples)*

Introduction *(by the Presider)*
Brothers and sisters, let us pray to God, who cares for all the flock.

Intercessions *(announced by the deacon, cantor or another person)*

1. For all who are part of the Christian family,
   that the love of God may inspire them. *(Pause for silent prayer)*   Lord, hear us.

2. For those who minister in the Church,
   that they may give freely of themselves as they proclaim the Kingdom.
   (Pause for silent prayer)   Lord, hear us.

3. For vocations to priesthood and religious life,
   that many may answer the call to serve. *(Pause for silent prayer)*   Lord, hear us.

4. For people with all kinds of diseases and sickness,
   that those who suffer may experience healing. *(Pause for silent prayer)*   Lord, hear us.

5. For students preparing for and sitting exams,
   that the gift of wisdom may be theirs. *(Pause for silent prayer)*   Lord, hear us.

6. For all the faithful departed,
   (especially N & N who died recently and N & N whose anniversaries occur),
   that they may enjoy life without end. *(Pause for silent prayer)*   Lord, hear us.

Conclusion *(by the Presider)*
God our Shepherd, you are faithful from age to age.
We bring all our prayers before you and ask your help, through Christ our Lord. Amen.

FOR LITURGY PLANNERS

Liturgical Suggestions
Penitential Rite c-viii. Alternative Opening Prayer. Preface of Sundays in Ordinary Time 7. Eucharistic Prayer 3. Solemn Blessing 11 (Ordinary Time 2)

Songs: 'Be Not Afraid'; 'Eagles' Wings'; 'Here I am, Lord'.

The Week Ahead
Monday 13 June: St Anthony of Padua, patron saint of lost items.
Tuesday 14 June: Shavu'ot (the Jewish Pentecost) ends at nightfall today.
Thursday 16 June: International Day of the African Child (UNICEF).
• *Next Sunday is celebrated as Father's Day in many countries.*

TWELFTH SUNDAY IN ORDINARY TIME

FOR PRESIDERS

Opening Comment
We have nothing to be afraid of, we're told in today's Gospel. God knows every one of our needs. We gather in God's presence to give thanks for this word of encouragement.
If Father's Day is celebrated, add:
On this Father's Day, we honour the presence and memory of our fathers – and all who have played a father's role.
> **Penitential Rite:** *To prepare ourselves for this celebration, we recall how much we rely on God's abundant grace (pause):*
> Lord Jesus, you raise us to new life: Lord, have mercy.
> Lord Jesus, you forgive us our sins: Christ, have mercy.
> Lord Jesus, you feed us with your body and blood: Lord, have mercy.

Introduction to the Scripture Readings
Jeremiah 20:10-13 – Jeremiah is 'under pressure', but still believes God is at his side, helping him.
Romans 5:12-15 – Sin affects everyone, according to St Paul, but grace comes to all through Christ.
Matthew 10:26-33 – Jesus reassures his followers and asks for their loyalty.

The General Intercessions *(Samples)*

> Introduction *(by the Presider)*
> God is full of love for us, so we are confident when we bring forward our prayers:

> Intercessions *(announced by the deacon, cantor or another person)*
> 1. For Christians persecuted for their faith in Christ,
>   that God's abundant grace may help them to persevere. *(Pause for silent prayer)*   Lord, hear us.
>
> 2. For those who serve us in public office,
>   that their dealings may be free from corruption, always above reproach.
>   *(Pause for silent prayer)*   Lord, hear us.
>
> 3. For people bound up by fear,
>   that Christ's comforting words may reassure them. *(Pause for silent prayer)*   Lord, hear us.
>
> 4. For those who suffer in mind or body,
>   that the gift of healing may be theirs. *(Pause for silent prayer)*   Lord, hear us.
>
> 5. For our fathers on this Father's Day,
>   that they may be blessed with good health – and that fathers who have died may have eternal rest.
>   *(Pause for silent prayer)*   Lord, hear us.
>
> 6. For all who have gone before us in faith,
>   (especially N & N who died recently and N & N whose anniversaries occur),
>   that they may be freed from the power of death, to live in God.
>   *(Pause for silent prayer)*   Lord, hear us.

> Conclusion *(by the Presider)*
> God of love and compassion, you listen to the needy when they cry to you:
> Turn towards us and give us your help, we pray, through Jesus Christ our Lord. Amen.

FOR LITURGY PLANNERS

Liturgical Suggestions
Penitential Rite c-vi. Alternative Opening Prayer. Preface of Sundays in Ordinary Time 8. Eucharistic Prayer 2. Solemn Blessing 12 (Ordinary Time 3). For Blessing for Fathers, please see the CCCB (Canadian) book of blessings, page 52.

Songs: 'Though The Mountains May Fall'; 'Be Not Afraid'; 'Our Father/Ár nAthair' (for Father's Day); 'Sweet Heart of Jesus'.

The Week Ahead
Monday 20 June: World Refugee Day.
Tuesday 21 June: Summer Solstice.
Thursday 23 June: St John's Eve (bonfire night). National Day in Luxembourg (the Grand Duke's Birthday).

THIRTEENTH SUNDAY IN ORDINARY TIME

FOR PRESIDERS

Opening Comment
We're told in today's readings that hospitality is a gift that brings a great reward. As we gather to thank God for the many gifts we've received, we ask for the grace to be hospitable to the visitors who will come our way this summer.

Penitential Rite: To begin, let us call to mind the times we failed to show love: (pause)
I confess...

Introduction to the Scripture Readings
2 Kings 4:8-11, 14-16 – A hospitable woman is rewarded for her kindness.
Romans 6:3-4, 8-11 – Paul reminds us why baptism is one of the greatest gifts we've been given.
Matthew 10:37-42 – Jesus describes the virtues good disciples must have, including hospitality.

The General Intercessions *(Samples)*

Introduction *(by the Presider)*
As God's people, gathered here to acclaim our king, we bring our prayers forward:

Intercessions *(announced by the deacon, cantor or another person)*

1. For those who have left everything to follow Christ,
   that they may have the courage to persevere in their vocation.
   (Pause for silent prayer)   Lord, hear us.

2. For homeless people, refugees and Travellers,
   that they may experience Christian hospitality. *(Pause for silent prayer)*   Lord, hear us.

3. For all who will visit our land this summer,
   that we may extend a Christian *'céad míle fáilte'* to them. *(Pause for silent prayer)*   Lord, hear us.

4. For those who experience loneliness,
   that our friendship may always support them. *(Pause for silent prayer)*   Lord, hear us.

5. For all the faithful departed,
   (especially N & N who died recently and N & N whose anniversaries occur),
   that their baptism may assure them of a place in the new life.
   (Pause for silent prayer)   Lord, hear us.

6. For our own needs, for those who have asked our prayers – whom we remember now:
   (Long pause for silent prayer)   Lord, hear us.

Conclusion *(by the Presider)*
We sing forever of your love, O Lord God,
and confidently bring our prayers to you, through Jesus Christ our Lord. Amen.

FOR LITURGY PLANNERS

Liturgical Suggestions
Penitential Rite b. Or, with the baptismal focus of the Second Reading in mind, begin with the Blessing and Sprinkling of Holy Water (page 387, Rite a). First Opening Prayer. Preface of Sundays in Ordinary Time 1. Eucharistic Prayer 3. Solemn Blessing 13 (Ordinary Time 4). The emphasis on a Christian welcome for strangers may be carried into the weekday Masses. The Mass prayers for refugees and exiles (Roman Missal page 835-836) are worth considering for such celebrations, with the matching Eucharistic Prayer.

Songs :'Be Thou My Vision'; 'Make me a Channel of your Peace'; 'This is my will'.

The Week Ahead
Tuesday 28 June: World War I Day (USA).
Wednesday 29 June: Sts Peter & Paul, the twin founders of the Church in Rome – and its patrons.
Friday 1 July: St Oliver Plunkett (First Friday). Also Canada Day.

FOURTEENTH SUNDAY IN ORDINARY TIME

FOR PRESIDERS

Opening Comment

There is much good news in today's Gospel. We're told we can bring all our troubles to Jesus and find rest. God will make our burden light. We praise God for the care promised us.

Penitential Rite: Let us call to mind the healing power of God, who takes away our sins: (pause)

Lord Jesus, you healed the sick: Lord, have mercy.

Lord Jesus, you forgave sinners: Christ have mercy.

Lord Jesus, you gave us yourself to heal us and bring us strength: Lord, have mercy.

Introduction to the Scripture Readings

Zechariah 9:9-10 – Peace will come, not through the instruments of worldly rulers, but through the gentleness of God.

Romans 8:9, 11-13 – Paul tells us that life is given to us through the gift of the Spirit, so we must not live unspiritual lives.

Matthew 11:25-30 – A promise of rest for the overburdened: Jesus refreshes and renews all who seek him.

The General Intercessions *(Samples)*

Introduction *(by the Presider)*

The Lord is kind and full of compassion, so we bring our prayers with confidence:

Intercessions *(announced by the deacon, cantor or another person)*

1. For Christian people everywhere,
   that they may learn to trust in God's gentle support. *(Pause for silent prayer)*   Lord, hear us.

2. For the leaders of all the nations,
   that their words and actions will lead to peace. *(Pause for silent prayer)*   Lord, hear us.

3. For those who live in parts of the world where there is war and division,
   (especially the people of...),
   that reconciliation may follow conflict. *(Pause for silent prayer)*   Lord, hear us.

4. For an end to hatred and hurt in the north of Ireland,
   that this year's marching season may pass off peacefully. *(Pause for silent prayer)*   Lord, hear us.

5. For all who labour and are overburdened,
   that they may experience the rest promised by Jesus. *(Pause for silent prayer)*   Lord, hear us.

6. For our brothers and sisters whose life on earth is over (especially N and N),
   that they may be raised to eternal life with Christ. *(Pause for silent prayer)*   Lord, hear us.

Conclusion *(by the Presider)*

God of compassion and faithfulness, you raise up all who are bowed down:

Hear the prayer we make to you this day, through Jesus Christ our Lord. Amen.

FOR LITURGY PLANNERS

Liturgical Suggestions

Penitential Rite c-viii. Alternative Opening Prayer. Preface of Sundays in Ordinary Time 7. Eucharistic Prayer 1. Solemn Blessing 14 (Ordinary Time 5). If continental visitors attend today, the presider might welcome them in their own language. Greetings in French follow; for other languages, please see the other July Sundays.

(In French): Chers amis qui venez passer vos vacances chez nous, nous sommes heureux de vous acceuillir parmi nous.

(Phonetically) 'Shares am-ee key venay passay vo va-kawnce shay noo, noo soms uru de vooz a-cow-year parmee noo.'

Songs:

'Be Still and Know that I am God'; 'Come to Me'; 'I will never Forget you my People'.

The Week Ahead

Monday 4 July: Independence Day (USA).

Tuesday 5 July: Tynwald Day (the Isle of Man's national day).

Friday 8 July: St Kilian, martyr, native of Ireland, venerated in Bavaria.

FIFTEENTH SUNDAY IN ORDINARY TIME

FOR PRESIDERS

Opening Comment

We gather as pilgrims on a journey, asking God to keep us steadfast until we reach our eternal home. In the Spirit, let us worship God who cares for us according to our needs.

Penitential Rite: Because the seeds of faith may not have fully taken root in our lives, let us call to mind our sins: I confess...

Introduction to the Scripture Readings

Isaiah 55:10-11 – The first reading and Gospel both describe the sowing of seeds of faith and the production of a successful crop in our lives.

Romans 8:18-23 – Paul tells us that our sufferings here can't be compared with the glory awaiting us.

Matthew 13:1-23 – Jesus uses the parable of the sower and explains it.

The General Intercessions *(Samples)*

Introduction *(by the Presider)*

My friends, the Lord crowns our lives with goodness, so we present our intercessions with confidence:

Intercessions *(announced by the deacon, cantor or another person)*

1. For the members of the Church,
   that their hearts may be always hear God's word and understand it.
   (Pause for silent prayer)   Lord, hear us.

2. For new converts to the Christian faith,
   that the Word of God may be firmly rooted in their lives. *(Pause for silent prayer)*   Lord, hear us.

3. For all whose faith is weak,
   that the love of God may make them what they are called to be.
   (Pause for silent prayer)   Lord, hear us.

4. For farmers and all who depend on the soil for their livelihood,
   that this year's crop may satisfy their needs. *(Pause for silent prayer)*   Lord, hear us.

5. For those who are far from home, for work or on holidays,
   that they may experience kindness, and travel in safety. *(Pause for silent prayer)*   Lord, hear us.

6. For all Irish people who have died in war or in the service of the United Nations,
   (and for N & N who died recently and N & N whose anniversaries occur),
   that they may share the glory awaiting all believers. *(Pause for silent prayer)*   Lord, hear us.

Conclusion *(by the Presider)*

God our creator, you provide for the earth and for all who live,
listen to the prayer we make to you today, through Christ our Lord. Amen.

FOR LITURGY PLANNERS

Liturgical Suggestions

Penitential rite a. Gospel (full form). Preface of Sundays in Ordinary Time 5. Eucharistic Prayer 3. Solemn Blessing 11 (Ordinary Time 2). If continental visitors attend today, the presider might welcome them in their own language. Greetings in German follow; for other languages, please see the other July Sundays.

(In German): 'Liebe Freunde, Sie kamen um Ihre Ferien hier zu verbringen. Wir freuen uns, Sie bei uns aufzunehmen.'

(Phonetically) 'Leeba froy-unda, zee cam-en um eere fair-ee-en here tsoo ver-bring-en. Veer froy-en unts, zee by unts owf-zoo-name-in.'

Songs: 'How Lovely on the Mountains'; 'Ag Críost an Síol'; 'Now Thank We All Our God'.

The Week Ahead

Monday 11 July: St Benedict, patron of Europe. World Population Day.

Tuesday 12 July: The Battle of the Boyne is remembered in the North of Ireland (Bank Holiday there).

Thursday 14 July: Bastille Day (National Day of France).

Friday 15 July: St Swithun, English bishop (Rain today means forty days of rain!)

SIXTEENTH SUNDAY IN ORDINARY TIME

FOR PRESIDERS

Opening Comment

We have been called together by the Spirit of God to celebrate the resurrection of the Lord Jesus. The Spirit teaches us to pray, and moves us to glorify the Lord's name.

Penitential Rite: To prepare ourselves for this celebration, let us call to mind our weakness and God's strength: (pause)
You raise the dead to life in the Spirit: Lord, have mercy.
You bring pardon and peace to the sinner: Christ, have mercy.
You bring light to those in darkness: Lord, have mercy.

Introduction to the Scripture Readings

Wisdom 12:13, 16-19 – God is a lenient judge, who understands our weakness.
Romans 8:26-27 – St Paul teaches that the Spirit comes to help us in our weakness.
Matthew: 24-43 – Within God's family there will always be faithful and unfaithful members, just as fields yield both wheat and weeds. God will sort them out at the end of time.

The General Intercessions *(Samples)*

Introduction *(by the Presider)*
Brothers and sisters, the Spirit helps us choose words to pray properly.
Open to the Spirit's help, let us bring our needs to the Father:

Intercessions *(announced by the deacon, cantor or another person)*

1. For all who try to live as Christians,
   that they may have the grace to rise above the evil around them.
   (Pause for silent prayer) — Lord, hear us.

2. For those who have never known faith,
   that the Good News of salvation may reach them. *(Pause for silent prayer)* — Lord, hear us.

3. For people who are finding life difficult at the moment,
   that the goodness of friends may reassure them of God's care.
   (Pause for silent prayer) — Lord, hear us.

4. For the young, as they search for truth,
   that the seed of faith sown in them may bear abundant fruit.
   (Pause for silent prayer) — Lord, hear us.

5. For those whose earthly journey is over (especially N & N),
   that our forgiving God may welcome them home. *(Pause for silent prayer)* — Lord, hear us.

Conclusion *(by the Presider)*
God of love and compassion, you do marvellous deeds:
Attend to the sound of our voice and take pity on us, we pray, through Christ our Lord. Amen.

FOR LITURGY PLANNERS

Liturgical Suggestions

Penitential Rite c-v. First Opening Prayer. Full form of Gospel provides a selection of images for the homily and an explanation of the first parable. (Shorter form: Matthew 13:24-30.) Preface of Sundays in Ordinary Time 8. Eucharistic Prayer 2. Solemn Blessing 12 (Ordinary Time 3). If continental visitors attend today, the presider might welcome them in their own language. Greetings in Italian follow; for other languages, please see the other July Sundays.

(In Italian): 'Cari amici, che venite a passare le vostre vacanza qui da noi, siamo felici di accogliervi nella nostra communità.'
(Phonetically) 'Caree amee-chee, kay vay-nee-tay ah pass-ah-ray lay voss-tray vah-can-za kwee da noy, see-amo fay-lee-chay day akol-ee-err-vee nellah noss-trah com-oo-nee-tah.'

Songs: 'How Great Thou Art'; 'Ag Críost an Síol'; 'Spirit of the Living God'.

The Week Ahead

Thursday 21 July: National Day of Belgium.
Friday 22 July: St Mary Magdalene is celebrated. Buddhist Lent begins today.
Saturday 23 July: St Bridget of Sweden, patron of Europe.

SEVENTEENTH SUNDAY IN ORDINARY TIME

FOR PRESIDERS

Opening Comment

God has given us many gifts, including the promise that we will share in Christ's glory. We give thanks for these treasures, as we continue on our journey to the fullness of the kingdom of heaven.

   Penitential rite: To prepare ourselves for this act of worship, let us call to mind our sins and God's faithfulness: (pause)

Lord Jesus, you have shown us the way to the Father: Lord, have mercy.

Lord Jesus, you have given us the consolation of the truth: Christ, have mercy.

Lord Jesus, you are the Good Shepherd, leading us into everlasting life: Lord, have mercy.

Introduction to the Scripture Readings

1 Kings 3:5, 7-12 – Solomon is offered any gift he chooses and opts for the gift of wisdom.

Romans 8:28-30 – Paul explains that God turns everything to good for those who love him.

Matthew 13:44-52 – Jesus describes the kingdom of heaven using many parables.

The General Intercessions *(Samples)*

   Introduction *(by the Presider)*

   Let us bring our prayers before our God of wisdom and love:

   Intercessions *(announced by the deacon, cantor or another person)*

1. That all Christians may be inspired to continue along the path to the Kingdom by the treasure that awaits them. *(Pause for silent prayer)*   Lord, hear us.

2. That those who govern nations may have the wisdom of the great leader Solomon. *(Pause for silent prayer)*   Lord, hear us.

3. That all who search for answers to their questions may receive the gift of true wisdom. *(Pause for silent prayer)*   Lord, hear us.

4. That those on pilgrimage may know the Lord's presence on their journey, particularly those reaching their goal at Compostela. *(Pause for silent prayer)*   Lord, hear us.

5. That those whose life on earth is over may reach their eternal home in heaven (especially N & N). *(Pause for silent prayer)*   Lord, hear us.

6. That we may have God's help in all our difficulties, particularly the needs we remember in silence now: *(Long pause for silent prayer)*   Lord, hear us.

   Conclusion *(by the Presider)*

   God of wisdom and love, your will is wonderful indeed:

   Hear the prayers we make and help us live by your precepts, through Christ our Lord. Amen.

FOR LITURGY PLANNERS

Liturgical Suggestions

Penitential Rite c-vii. First opening prayer. The shorter form of the Gospel may be used (Matthew 13:44-46). Preface of Sundays in Ordinary Time 6. Eucharistic Prayer 3. Solemn Blessing 13 (Ordinary Time 4). If continental visitors attend today, the presider might welcome them in their own language. Greetings in Spanish follow; for other languages, please see the other July Sundays.

(In Spanish): *'Quiero dar una bienvenida muy especial a los visitantes españoles. Deseo que tengan unas vaccaciones felices entre nosotros.*
(Phonetically) '*Ki-er-oh dar oona be-en-ven-eeda mo-ee espes-ee-al a lows visi-tant-eys e-span-yole-es.*
Des-ay-o kay ten-gan oon-as vack-ass-ee-owen-es fe-lee-th-es en-tray nose-ot-rose.'

Songs: 'Lord of All Hopefulness'; 'Be Not Afraid'; 'Go Tell Everyone'.

The Week Ahead

Monday 25 July: St James, patron of Spain, where devotion is centred on Santiago de Compostela.
Tuesday 26 July: Sts Joachim and Anne, parents of Mary, grandparents of Jesus.
Saturday 30 July: Father-in-law Day (USA).

EIGHTEENTH SUNDAY IN ORDINARY TIME

FOR PRESIDERS

Opening Comment

Great wonders are proclaimed in today's Liturgy. God's love and God's care for humanity are made manifest.

Penitential rite: As we accept God's invitation to a feast, we remember the sins he promises to take away: (pause)
Lord Jesus, you raise us to new life: Lord, have mercy.
Lord Jesus, you forgive us our sins: Christ, have mercy.
Lord Jesus, you feed us with your body and blood: Lord, have mercy.

Introduction to the Scripture Readings

Isaiah 55:1-3 – Contains the Lord's invitation to those in need to have their thirst satisfied.
Romans 8:35, 37-39 – Paul beautifully describes the boundless love of Christ.
Matthew 14:13-21 – Jesus sees to it that the hungry are fed, despite his own grief at the death of John the Baptist.

The General Intercessions *(Samples)*

Introduction *(by the Presider)*
The Lord is kind and full of compassion, so we bring our prayers to God in confidence:

Intercessions *(announced by the deacon, cantor or another person)*

1. For all the members of the Church,
    that we may grow in appreciation of God's kindness. *(Pause for silent prayer)*   Lord, hear us.

2. For those who suffer persecution for what they believe,
    that men and women of goodwill may defend their rights. *(Pause for silent prayer)* Lord, hear us.

3. For the people who hunger and thirst in a world of plenty,
    that Christians may reflect God's generosity by continuing to share.
    (Pause for silent prayer)   Lord, hear us.

4. For people who are travelling, on holidays or on pilgrimage,
    that they may travel safely and come home refreshed. *(Pause for silent prayer)* Lord, hear us.

5. For those who have died (especially N & N) and all who have been lost in road accidents,
    that the grieving may realise that nothing can separate us from God's love.
    (Pause for silent prayer)   Lord, hear us.

6. For the members of this community who are in any kind of need,
    and our own needs, which we remember now. *(Long pause for silent prayer)*   Lord, hear us.

Conclusion *(by the Presider)*
God our creator, you are close to all who call on you from their hearts:
Continue to show us your compassion and love, we pray, through Jesus Christ our Lord. Amen.

FOR LITURGY PLANNERS

Liturgical Suggestions

Penitential Rite c-vi. Alternative Opening Prayer. Preface of Sundays in Ordinary Time 7. Eucharistic Prayer 2. Communion under both species would reflect the divine generosity in today's Gospel. Solemn Blessing 10 (Ordinary Time 1). If continental visitors attend today, the presider might welcome them in their own language. Greetings in Dutch follow; for other languages, please see the other July Sundays.
(In Dutch): 'Beste vrienden, die bij ons uw verlof komt doorbrengen, wij zijn blij u hier te begroeten
(Phonetically) 'Best-eh freend-en, dee by uns oo fer-lof come-teh door-breng-en, vigh zine bligh oo here tuh buh-ghroot-in.'

Songs: 'The King of Love my Shepherd is'; 'Take and Eat'; 'Colours of Day'.

The Week Ahead

Monday 1 August: Lammas (or 'Loaf-Mass') Day, the start of the ancient harvest festival. Bank Holiday.
Thursday 4 August: St John Vianney (the Curé of Ars), patron of priests.
Saturday 6 August: The Transfiguration of the Lord. Anniversary of the dropping of the atomic bomb on Hiroshima (1945) and of the death of Pope Paul VI (1978).

NINETEENTH SUNDAY IN ORDINARY TIME

FOR PRESIDERS

Opening Comment

We gather to celebrate our beautiful God, who was revealed to Elijah as a gentle breeze and who calmed the storm on the lake. We are grateful that this God takes our fears away and gives rest to our souls.

Penitential Rite: Remembering God's enduring mercy, let us call to mind our sins...

Lord Jesus, you came to reconcile us to one another and to the Father: Lord, have mercy.

Lord Jesus, you heal the wounds of sin and division: Christ, have mercy.

Lord Jesus, you intercede for us with your Father: Lord, have mercy.

Introduction to the Scripture Readings

Isaiah 56:1, 6-7 – God is a calming presence in both the First Reading and Gospel today. In this reading, Elijah finds God not in the storm but in the gentle breeze.

Romans 9:1-5 – Paul acknowledges the role of the Jews in the salvation history. He would do anything to help them see this.

Matthew 14:22-33 – Jesus shows us that when we keep our eyes on him, none of life's storms can hurt us.

The General Intercessions *(Samples)*

Introduction *(by the Presider)*

God's help is near for those who believeve, so we can present our petitions with confidence.

Intercessions *(announced by the deacon, cantor or another person)*

1. That all who are part of the Christian family
    may find strength in praying to our God of gentleness and calm.
    (Pause for silent prayer)   Lord, hear us.

2. That the nations who live in mistrust of each other
    may learn to resolve their differences peacefully. *(Pause for silent prayer)*   Lord, hear us.

3. That all who go to sea, for work or leisure,
    may be spared from violent storms. *(Pause for silent prayer)*   Lord, hear us.

4. That those who staff the lifeboats, and take part in search and rescue missions,
    may themselves enjoy God's protection. *(Pause for silent prayer)*   Lord, hear us.

5. That all the members of this community
    may know Christ's calming presence in the troubles of life. *(Pause for silent prayer)*   Lord, hear us.

6. That the dead, particularly those who have been lost at sea,
    may know the calm peace of the Father's House. (We also remember N who died recently
    and N & N whose anniversaries occur – *Pause for silent prayer)*   Lord, hear us.

Conclusion *(by the Presider)*

O God, our help and our refuge, you guide your people according to your wisdom:
Accept our prayers and come to our aid, through Christ our Lord. Amen.

FOR LITURGY PLANNERS

Liturgical Suggestions

Penitential Rite: c-iv. First Opening Prayer. The first reading emphasises God's presence in silence; leave some moments for quiet prayer. Preface of Sundays in Ordinary Time 1. Eucharistic Prayer 1. Solemn Blessing 14 (Ordinary Time 5). If continental visitors attend today, the presider might welcome them in their own language at the start of Mass. (Greetings given on pages 55 to 59)

Songs: 'Christ Be Beside Me'; 'Be Not Afraid'; 'Glory and Praise to our God'.

The Week Ahead

Monday 8 August: St Dominic, patron of preachers.

Thursday 11 August: St Clare of Assisi, patron of television. Chinese Valentine's Day.

Friday 12 August: International Youth Day (UN).

TWENTIETH SUNDAY IN ORDINARY TIME

FOR PRESIDERS

Opening Comment

Everyone is welcome in God's house, everyone who loves God's name. We gather to experience the warmth of this embrace.

Penitential Rite: To prepare ourselves, let us call to mind our sins, remembering God's compassion for sinners: (pause)
Lord Jesus, you came to gather the nations into the peace of God's kingdom: Lord, have mercy.
You come in word and sacrament to strengthen us in holiness: Christ, have mercy.
You will come in glory with salvation for your people: Lord, have mercy.

Introduction to the Scripture Readings

Isaiah 56:1, 6-7 – God's laws are simple to understand: even foreigners can live by them. Our God is the God of all people.
Romans 11:13-15, 29-32 – Paul longs to see the Jews realise that Jesus is their Messiah, even though he admits God's plan is beyond our understanding.
Matthew 15:21-28 – The Canaanite woman was persistent, a reminder that persistent faith is fruitful.

The General Intercessions *(Samples)*

Introduction *(by the Presider)*
God sheds his light on us, so we bring our prayers with confidence:

Intercessions *(announced by the deacon, cantor or another person)*

1. That people of every nation, race, colour and religion
    may be united in working for justice and integrity. *(Pause for silent prayer)*   Lord, hear us.

2. That those who follow Christ
    may never forget that all are welcome on God's holy mountain.
    (Pause for silent prayer)   Lord, hear us.

3. That in our daily lives
    we may show love to the people from other countries who live in our midst.
    (Pause for silent prayer)   Lord, hear us.

4. That those who receive exam results at this time of year,
    may find happiness in life, with a deep faith to guide them. *(Pause for silent prayer)* Lord, hear us.

5. That all who suffer, in mind, body or spirit,
    may experience Christ's healing power. *(Pause for silent prayer)*   Lord, hear us.

6. For our brothers and sisters who have died (especially N & N)
    that they may come to God's holy mountain, along with those whose faith is known to God alone.
    (Pause for silent prayer)   Lord, hear us.

Conclusion *(by the Presider)*
Gracious God, all the nations find their help in you:
Teach us to trust in your love as you grant our petitions, through Jesus Christ our Lord. Amen.

FOR LITURGY PLANNERS

Liturgical Suggestions

Penitential Rite: c-ii. Eucharistic Prayer 4 (with its own preface). Solemn Blessing 11 (Ordinary Time 2). If continental visitors attend today, the presider might welcome them in their own language at the start of Mass. (Greetings given on pages 55 to 59)

Songs: 'All the Ends of the Earth'; 'Glory and Praise to our God'; 'Sing a New Song'.

The Week Ahead

Monday 15 August: The Assumption of Our Lady (holyday of obligation). Mother's Day in Costa Rica.
Tuesday 16 August: Anniversary of the death of Elvis Presley.
Saturday 20 August: St Bernard of Clairvaux, composer of the 'Memorare', patron saint of Gibraltar.

ASSUMPTION OF THE BVM

FOR PRESIDERS

Opening Comment
We worship God who brought Mary to the glory of heaven this day.
We celebrate her Assumption, the tangible reminder that the resurrection of Jesus brings victory over death for all who believe.
Penitential Rite: To prepare ourselves to celebrate this great feast, let us call to mind our sins: (pause)
Lord Jesus, you are mighty God and Prince of Peace: Lord, have mercy.
Lord Jesus, you are Son of God and Son of Mary: Christ, have mercy.
Lord Jesus, you are Word made flesh and splendour of the Father: Lord, have mercy.

Introduction to the Scripture Readings (Vigil Mass)
1 Chronicles 15:3-4, 15-16; 16:1-2 – Describes David honouring the ark of the covenant. Mary is the new Ark of the Covenant.
1 Corinthians 15:54-57 – We have victory over death in Jesus. We share this joy with Mary.
Luke 11:27-28 – Being related to Jesus is not as important as doing God's will, as Mary did.

Introduction to the Scripture Readings (Mass during the Day)
Apocalypse 11:19; 12:1-6, 10 – Symbolically describes Christ being born into a dangerous world as Mary's child, to win victory over evil.
1 Corinthians 15:20-26 – Paul reminds us that the death of Jesus guarantees we will all share in the resurrection, as Mary already does.
Luke 1:39-56 – The Magnificat is Mary's song of praise for all the good things God has done.

The General Intercessions *(Samples)*

> **Introduction** *(by the Presider)*
> Let us bring our prayers before God, who does great things for all people.

> **Intercessions** *(announced by the deacon, cantor or another person)*
> 1. For the leaders of the Church,
>   that they may always believe and teach the Good News about life without end.
>   *(Pause for silent prayer)* Lord, hear us.
>
> 2. For those who fear that death extinguishes all life,
>   that Mary's assumption may reinforce their hope. *(Pause for silent prayer)* Lord, hear us.
>
> 3. For all in need of healing, of mind or body,
>   that Mary's prayers may sustain them. *(Pause for silent prayer)* Lord, hear us.
>
> 4. For those who are very ill and near death,
>   that they may realise they have the support of this community's prayers. *(Pause)* Lord, hear us.
>
> 5. For our friends whose life in this world is over (especially N & N),
>   and for those who died at Omagh, seven years ago today:
>   that all the dead may join Mary and the saints in the glory of heaven. *(Pause)* Lord, hear us.

> **Conclusion** *(by the Presider)*
> Almighty God, you come to the help of your servants in their need,
> hear the prayers we make in faith, through Christ our Lord. Amen.

FOR LITURGY PLANNERS

Liturgical Suggestions
Penitential Rite: c-iii. Alternative Opening Prayer. Preface of the Assumption. Eucharistic Prayer 2. Solemn Blessing 15 (The Blessed Virgin Mary). If continental visitors attend today, the presider might welcome them in their own language at the start of Mass. (Greetings given on pages 55 to 59)

Songs: 'When Creation Was Begun'; 'Hail Queen of Heaven'; any version of the Magnificat.

TWENTY-FIRST SUNDAY IN ORDINARY TIME

FOR PRESIDERS

Opening Comment
This hour of worship brings us into the presence of the God whose mystery we can never comprehend. All we have comes from the Lord, and we can only bow down in awe, and bring forward the praise that is due to the Almighty.

Penitential Rite: To prepare ourselves for the worship of God, let us call to mind our sins: (pause)
I confess…

Introduction to the Scripture Readings
Isaiah 22:19-23 – God exercises his authority, removing one leader and replacing him with another.
Romans 11:33-36 – Paul reminds us that God is beyond our understanding, that no one can claim to have figured out the mind of God.
Matthew 116:13-20 – Peter is given authority on the basis of his act of faith.

The General Intercessions *(Samples)*

Introduction *(by the Presider)*
Let us bring our prayers into God's presence, remembering that God's love for us is eternal.

Intercessions *(announced by the deacon, cantor or another person)*

1. For our Pope N, and our bishop N,
   that they may preach God's word with wisdom and faith. *(Pause for silent prayer)* Lord, hear us.

2. For all in positions of authority, in Church and State,
   that they may serve with humility and gentleness. *(Pause for silent prayer)* Lord, hear us.

3. For those who have suffered through the abuse of power,
   that healing and new strength may be theirs. *(Pause for silent prayer)* Lord, hear us.

4. For people who travel on pilgrimage, to Knock and the other great shrines,
   that they may travel safely and return home refreshed. *(Pause for silent prayer)* Lord, hear us.

5. For the leaders of the Church who have died, and all the faithful departed (especially N & N),
   that they may join their saintly predecessors in the Father's house.
   (Pause for silent prayer) Lord, hear us.

6. For our own needs, for those who have asked our prayers – whom we remember now:
   (Long pause for silent prayer) Lord, hear us.

Conclusion *(by the Presider)*
God of love, you never discard the work of your hands:
Hear the prayers we make to you, in trust, through Christ our Lord. Amen.

FOR LITURGY PLANNERS

Liturgical Suggestions
Penitential Rite a (Confiteor). Alternative opening prayer. Preface of Sundays in Ordinary Time 4 and Eucharistic Prayer 2. Solemn Blessing 12 (Ordinary Time 3) or 17 (The Apostles: 'May God… bless you through the prayers of Saint Peter.') If continental visitors attend today, the presider might welcome them in their own language at the start of Mass. (Greetings given on pages 55 to 59)

Songs: 'Be Thou My Vision'; 'Immortal, Invisible, God Only Wise'; 'Be Not Afraid'.

The Week Ahead
Tuesday 23 August: International Day for the Remembrance of the Slave Trade and Its Abolition (UN).
Friday 26 August: Women's Equality Day (USA).
Saturday 27 August: St Monica, mother of St Augustine (patron of mothers).

TWENTY-SECOND SUNDAY IN ORDINARY TIME

FOR PRESIDERS

Opening Comment

We gather to praise God and to ask for help and grace. We know the difficulties that can come when we try to live the right way. Often the road of life is like the way of the cross.

Penitential Rite: Let us call to mind our moments of failure, conscious that God's grace raises us up: (pause)
Lord Jesus, you raise us to new life: Lord, have mercy.
Lord Jesus, you forgive us our sins: Christ, have mercy.
Lord Jesus, you feed us with your body and blood: Lord, have mercy.

Introduction to the Scripture Readings

Jeremish 20:7-9 – Jeremiah describes the difficulties preaching the word brought him.
Romans 12:1-2 – Paul believes we must offer our bodies as a living sacrifice to God.
Matthew 16:21-27 – Jesus warns of the suffering discipleship will involve.

The General Intercessions *(Samples)*

Introduction *(by the Presider)*
Brothers and sisters, let us bring our prayers to God, who has always been our help.

Intercessions *(announced by the deacon, cantor or another person)*

1.   For Christians who suffer persecution for their faith,
     that they may hold firm in the face of every trial. *(Pause for silent prayer)*   Lord, hear us.

2.   For all those who endure criticism for doing what they believe is right,
     that they may have the courage to persevere. *(Pause for silent prayer)*   Lord, hear us.

3.   For the grace to support our fellow pilgrims in the hardships of life:
     that we may become more aware of each other's sufferings.
     (Pause for silent prayer)   Lord, hear us.

4.   For all who struggle with illness, of mind or body,
     that their way of the cross may bring them to glory. *(Pause for silent prayer)*   Lord, hear us.

5.   For our own needs, for those who have asked our prayers –
     especially those we remember now. *(Long pause for silent prayer)*   Lord, hear us.

6.   For the faithful departed (especially N & N),
     that sharing the cross of Christ they may also share his victory over death.
     (Pause for silent prayer)   Lord, hear us.

Conclusion *(by the Presider)*
O Lord our God, your love is better than life:
Come to our help, we pray, through Jesus Christ our Lord. Amen.

FOR LITURGY PLANNERS

Liturgical Suggestions

Highlight the cross today, by carrying it in the entrance procession and incensing it. Penitential Rite c-vi. Alternative opening prayer. Preface of Sundays in Ordinary Time 2. Eucharistic Prayer 3. Solemn Blessing 5 (The Passion of the Lord). If continental visitors attend today, the presider might welcome them in their own language at the start of Mass. (Greetings given on pages 55 to 59).

Songs: 'Christ Be Beside Me'; 'The King of Love My Shepherd Is'; 'O the Love of My Lord is the Essence'.

The Week Ahead

Monday 29 August: Summer Bank Holiday (GB and NI).
Tuesday 30 August: St Fiacre, patron saint of gardeners.
Thursday 1 September: Lailat al Miraj (Ascension of the Prophet – Islam).

HARVEST THANKSGIVING

FOR PRESIDERS

Opening Comment

We gather this autumn time to give thanks to God for feeding people in town and country alike through the marvels of creation. We believe that those who trust in God's providence are not disappointed, but are fed from the abundance of divine riches.

Penitential Rite: Delighting in God's care, let us call to mind moments of doubt and weakness: (pause)

Lord Jesus, you raise us to new life: Lord, have mercy.

Lord Jesus, you forgive us our sins: Christ, have mercy.

Lord Jesus, you feed us with your body and blood: Lord, have mercy.

Introduction to the Scripture Readings

Joel 2:21-24, 26-27 – When harvest time comes, God's people will not be disappointed;

1 Corinthians 3:6-10 – People labour to produce the harvest, but God is behind it all.

Luke 17:11-19 – Saying 'thank you' may be rarely done, but it is always appreciated – even by the Lord.

The General Intercessions *(Samples)*

Introduction *(by the Presider)*

Brothers and sisters, we gather at the fall of the year to give praise for we have received.

Let us bring our prayers to God, who will always be our help.

Intercessions *(announced by the deacon, cantor or another person)*

1. For farmers, fishermen and all who work to put food on our tables,
   that they may see the creator's hand at work in all that they do.
   (Pause for silent prayer)   Lord, hear us.

2. For those who process our food, transport it and serve it for us,
   that they may know their role in God's plan for the world. *(Pause for silent prayer)*   Lord, hear us.

3. For people who suffer from hunger and thirst in many countries,
   that those with plenty to eat and drink may never fail to share.
   (Pause for silent prayer)   Lord, hear us.

4. For the members of our comunity who are in any kind of need,
   that we may make God's care known through our words and deeds.
   (Pause for silent prayer)   Lord, hear us.

5. For the dead, for all who have passed on since last year's harvest,
   that they may share joyfully in the banquet of heaven. *(Pause for silent prayer)*   Lord, hear us.

6. A moment's quiet prayer for our own particular needs of today.
   (Long pause for silent prayer)   Lord, hear us.

Conclusion *(by the Presider)*

God our creator, you never fail to provide for all your creatures:

Hear the prayers we make in faith and trust, through Jesus Christ our Lord. Amen.

FOR LITURGY PLANNERS

Liturgical Suggestions

Involve relevant local people in planning this liturgy: in rural areas, members of organisations like the IFA or Macra might participate. Invite schoolchildren to take part in decorating the church for the celebration, reflecting all the elements of creation.

Penitential Rite c-vi. Mass prayers for 'After The Harvest', Roman Missal pages 832 to 833, or 'Thanksgiving', pages 844 to 845. Readings from Lectionary Volume III, pages 642 to 648, or from the 'Thanksgiving' selection (686-700).

If Mass is celebrated: Preface of Weekdays IV. Eucharistic Prayer 2. Solemn Blessing 11 (Ordinary Time 2).

Songs: 'Holy God, We Praise Thy Name'; 'Sing a New Song Unto the Lord'; 'Now Thank We All Our God'.

TWENTY-THIRD SUNDAY IN ORDINARY TIME

FOR PRESIDERS

Opening Comment

We gather as God's family, concerned for each other, supporting one another in sadness and joy. The challenge of living as part of the Christian family is laid out for us in today's readings.

Penitential Rite: At times we fail to show love, so as we make a new start at this time of year, we ask forgiveness: (pause) I confess...

Introduction to the Scripture Readings

Ezekiel 33:7-9 – God tells Ezekiel he will be held accountable for his task as a prophet.
Romans 13:8-10 – Paul insists that what is done in love cannot hurt another.
Matthew 18:15-20 – Jesus shows how love can sometimes include confrontation.

The General Intercessions *(Samples)*

Introduction *(by the Presider)*
As members of God's flock, let us confidently bring forward our prayers:

Intercessions *(announced by the deacon, cantor or another person)*

1. For the prophets called to challenge God's people,
    that they may never be afraid to speak the truth. *(Pause for silent prayer)*   Lord, hear us.

2. For all the members of the Church,
    that we may courageously help each other to become more Christian.
    (Pause for silent prayer)   Lord, hear us.

3. For those who live close to us,
    that our neighbours may receive love and understanding from us.
    (Pause for silent prayer)   Lord, hear us.

4. For all who are returning to school, students and teachers alike,
    that they may have gifts of wisdom and understanding. *(Pause for silent prayer)*   Lord, hear us.

5. For those who have gone before us in faith (especially N & N),
    that the Good Shepherd may include them in the heavenly flock.
    (Pause for silent prayer)   Lord, hear us.

6. For our own needs, for those who have asked our prayers –
    especially those we remember now. *(Long pause for silent prayer)*   Lord, hear us.

Conclusion *(by the Presider)*
O God our creator, you are the rock who saves us:
Listen to our voice and help us in our needs, through Christ our Lord. Amen.

FOR LITURGY PLANNERS

Liturgical Suggestions

Penitential Rite a (Confiteor). Or the Rite could be replaced with the Blessing and Sprinkling of Holy Water, to mark the new beginning September brings (texts given before the Penitential Rite in the Roman Missal). First opening prayer. Preface of Sundays in Ordinary Time 8. Eucharistic Prayer 1. Solemn Blessing 14 (Ordinary Time 5) or Blessing 3, for the Beginning of the New (School) Year.

Songs: 'Love is His Word'; 'Ag Críost an Síol'; 'This is My Will'.

The Week Ahead

Monday 5 September: Month of Elul begins in Judaism (time of repentance before Rosh Hashanah and Yom Kippur.)
Thursday 8 September: Birthday of the Blessed Virgin Mary. International Literacy Day (UN).
Friday 9 September: Blessed Frederick Ozanam, founder of the St Vincent de Paul Society.
• *Next Sunday (the second Sunday of September) is Racial Justice Sunday. (Also: Grandparents' Day in the US.)*

TWENTY-FOURTH SUNDAY IN ORDINARY TIME

FOR PRESIDERS

Opening Comment

Forgiveness is one of the great qualities of Christianity. We are challenged to forgive each other as readily as God forgives us. We celebrate God's mercy, and ask for the grace to pass it on to those who hurt us.

Penitential Rite: Remembering that God's mercy is the source of all forgiveness, let us call to mind our need of it:
Lord Jesus, you came to reconcile us to one another and to the Father: Lord, have mercy.
Lord Jesus, you heal the wounds of sin and division: Christ, have mercy.
Lord Jesus, you intercede for us with your Father: Lord, have mercy.

Introduction to the Scripture Readings

Ecclesiasticus 27:30 to 28:7 – Both the first reading and Gospel invite us to be merciful and forgiving to each other, as God is towards us. If we nurse anger, how can we expect compassion?
Romans 14:7-9 – Paul tells us the good news that, whether alive or dead, we belong to the Lord.
Matthew 18:21-35 – The Gospel has a sting in the tail: if we fail in forgiveness, we risk being judged according to our own standards.

The General Intercessions *(Samples)*

Introduction *(by the Presider)*
The Lord is compassion and love, so we present our prayers with confidence:

Intercessions *(announced by the deacon, cantor or another person)*

1. For forgiveness among Christians,
    that we may treat each other as God treats us. *(Pause for silent prayer)*   Lord, hear us.

2. For an end to vengenace and hatred,
    that all people may learn to live together in tolerance. *(Pause for silent prayer)*   Lord, hear us.

3. For sports men and women, on this All-Ireland Sunday,
    that true sporting values may inspire Irish people everywhere.
    (Pause for silent prayer)   Lord, hear us.

4. For our community, as parish activities resume after the summer break,
    that God may be with us as we make a new start together. *(Pause for silent prayer)* Lord, hear us.

5. For the people of the United States, still grieving those lost in the attacks of
    11 September 2001, and for all those who died on that day and in the violence since,
    that the Lord may keep them in his loving care. *(Pause for silent prayer)*   Lord, hear us.

6. For our friends who died recently (N & N) and for all those whose anniversaries occur (N & N)
    that they may share in the eternal redemption won by Christ.
    (Pause for silent prayer)   Lord, hear us.

Conclusion *(by the Presider)*
God of mercy and compassion, you heal every one of our ills:
Help us, we pray you, through Jesus Christ our Lord. Amen.

FOR LITURGY PLANNERS

Liturgical Suggestions

Highlight forgiveness in today's liturgy by emphasising the Sign of Peace and the Our Father. (Use Introduction C: 'Let us ask our Father to forgive our sins and to…') Penitential Rite c-iv. First opening prayer. Eucharistic Prayer of Reconciliation 1 (with its own preface). Or Preface of Sundays 5 and Eucharistic Prayer 2. Solemn Blessing 13 (Ordinary Time 4).

Songs: 'Blest be the Lord'; 'Grant to us O Lord'; 'Love is His Word'.

The Week Ahead

Wednesday 14 September: The Triumph of the Cross.
Friday 16 September: International Day for the Preservation of the Ozone Layer (UN). Independence Day (Mexico).
Saturday 17 September: Citizenship Day (USA).

TWENTY-FIFTH SUNDAY IN ORDINARY TIME

FOR PRESIDERS

Opening Comment

God's ways are not our ways. God's love and generosity are beyond our understanding. We acknowledge all God has done for us, and ask for the grace to grow into God's likeness.

Penitential Rite: To prepare ourselves to celebrate the generosity of God, let us remember our need of divine help: (pause)
You raise the dead to life in the Spirit: Lord, have mercy.
You bring pardon and peace to the sinner: Christ, have mercy.
You bring light to those in darkness: Lord, have mercy.

Introduction to the Scripture Readings

Isaiah 55:6-9 – Both the first reading and Gospel remind us that God's generosity exceeds our expectations. As high as the heavens are above the earth are God's ways different from ours, proclaims Isaiah.
Philippians 1:20-24, 27 – Paul tells us that Christ means everything to him.
Matthew 20:1-16 – Jesus uses a story to show that God makes individual arrangements with each of his servants.

The General Intercessions *(Samples)*

Introduction *(by the Presider)*
The Lord is close to all who call, so we ask for help in our needs:

Intercessions *(announced by the deacon, cantor or another person)*

1. For all who follow the Christian way,
    that they may learn to rejoice in God's boundless generosity.
    (Pause for silent prayer)   Lord, hear us.

2. For this community,
    that all may find a welcome here, newcomers and longtime residents alike.
    (Pause for silent prayer)   Lord, hear us.

3. For workers and those who employ others,
    that industrial peace may result from the rights of all being respected.
    (Pause for silent prayer)   Lord, hear us.

4. For those who cannot find work,
    that their needs may not be forgotten. *(Pause for silent prayer)*   Lord, hear us.

5. For all the sick, particularly those coming to the end of their earthly life,
    that they may experience comfort on the journey to their Father's house.
    (Pause for silent prayer)   Lord, hear us.

6. For those who gone before us in faith (especially N & N),
    that the Lord's generosity may assure them of a place in the kingdom.
    (Pause for silent prayer)   Lord, hear us.

Conclusion *(by the Presider)*
God of kindness and compassion, you are close to all who call upon you:
Hear the prayers we make to you, through Christ our Lord. Amen.

FOR LITURGY PLANNERS

Liturgical Suggestions

Penitential Rite c-v. Or replace it with the Blessing and Sprinkling of Holy Water, with prayer B. Alternative opening prayer. Preface of Sundays in Ordinary Time 7. Eucharistic Prayer 3. Solemn Blessing 12 (Ordinary Time 3).

Songs: 'Be Thou my Vision'; 'Ag Críost an Síol'; 'Now Thank We All Our God'.

The Week Ahead

Monday 19 September: Respect for the Elderly Day (Japan).
Wednesday 21 September: International Day of Peace (UN). Autumnal equinox.
Friday 23 September: Padre Pio (St Pius of Pietrelcina)

TWENTY-SIXTH SUNDAY IN ORDINARY TIME

FOR PRESIDERS

Opening Comment

God's love is displayed for us in the life and death of Jesus. We rejoice in this love, and celebrate the victory over sin and death won for us. As a community, we praise God's holy name.

> *Penitential Rite: Sometimes our words and actions do not match each other. We call to mind our sins: (pause)* I confess...

Introduction to the Scripture Readings

Ezekiel 18:25-28 – Ezekiel reminds us that our actions have consequences.

Philippians 2:1-11 – Contains Paul's ancient hymn to Christ, which is read each year during the liturgy of Palm Sunday.

Matthew 21: 28-32 – Jesus teaches us that God wants our full commitment, not lip-service.

The General Intercessions *(Samples)*

Introduction *(by the Presider)*

The Lord's mercy never ends, so we present our prayers with confidence.

Intercessions *(announced by the deacon, cantor or another person)*

1. For the leaders of the Church,
    that they may sincerely and fully live the message they preach.
    (Pause for silent prayer)   Lord, hear us.

2. For people who feel they are beyond God's mercy,
    that they may know the welcome extended to those who change their ways.
    (Pause for silent prayer)   Lord, hear us.

3. For all who are on the margins of society, for men and women who are exploited,
    that justice and equality may prevail in our land. *(Pause for silent prayer)*   Lord, hear us.

4. For those who endure sickness, in mind or body,
    that the support of friends may remind them of God's healing care.
    (Pause for silent prayer)   Lord, hear us.

5. For all who have suffered death (especially N & N),
    that they may be raised to life through Jesus' resurrection.
    (Pause for silent prayer)   Lord, hear us.

6. For a moment, we remember in silence our own particular needs...
    (Long pause for silent prayer)   Lord, hear us.

Conclusion *(by the Presider)*

O God of endless goodness, your love and mercy have no end:
Hear the prayers your people make in faith, through Christ our Lord. Amen.

FOR LITURGY PLANNERS

Liturgical Suggestions

Penitential Rite a (Confiteor). Alternative opening prayer. Second reading (full form). Preface of Sundays in Ordinary Time 6. Eucharistic Prayer 2. Solemn Blessing 10 (Sundays in Ordinary Time 1).

Songs: 'Here I Am, Lord'; 'Be Not Afraid'; 'The King of Love My Shepherd is'.

The Week Ahead

Thursday 29 September: Michaelmas Day. (Traditional 'quarter day' in Ireland and England.)

Friday 30 September: St Jerome (patron of librarians).

Saturday 1 October: International Day for the Elderly (UN).

TWENTY-SEVENTH SUNDAY IN ORDINARY TIME

FOR PRESIDERS

Opening Comment

There are reassuring words for us in God's Word, with Paul reminding us that there is no need for us to worry. If there is anything we need, we can pray for it and God's peace will be ours.

Penitential Rite: Confident in this divine care, we remember our sins in the light of God's mercy (pause):
Lord Jesus, you have shown us the way to the Father: Lord, have mercy.
Lord Jesus, you have given us the consolation of the truth: Christ, have mercy.
Lord Jesus, you are the Good Shepherd, leading us into everlasting life: Lord, have mercy.

Introduction to the Scripture Readings

Isaiah 5:1-7 – God poetically recounts all he has done for his people, and shows sadness and anger at what he has got in return.
Philippians 4:6-9 – Peace is promised for all who ask God's help.
Matthew 21:33-43 – The sadness of the first reading is reflected in the Gospel: this time there is disappointment at how God's son is treated.

The General Intercessions *(Samples)*

Introduction *(by the Presider)*
Let us bring our prayers into the presence of the Lord of hosts, who promises peace to those who pray.

Intercessions *(announced by the deacon, cantor or another person)*

1. For all the members of the Church,
    that we may be thankful for what we have been given. *(Pause for silent prayer)* Lord, hear us.

2. For those who lead countries and governments,
    that they may respect human life and work to defend it. *(Pause for silent prayer)* Lord, hear us.

3. For all men and women of goodwill,
    that they may uphold the sacredness of human life from beginning to end.
    (Pause for silent prayer)   Lord, hear us.

4. For people who worry, and for all who suffer,
    that the peace of God may fill them. *(Pause for silent prayer)*   Lord, hear us.

5. For those who have died (especially N & N), and all who mourn after them.
    that eternal peace and comfort may be theirs. *(Pause for silent prayer)*   Lord, hear us.

6. A moment's quiet prayer for all our needs *(Long pause for silent prayer)*   Lord, hear us.

Conclusion *(by the Presider)*
God of hosts, you turn your face to your people:
Let your grace fill us according to our needs, through Christ our Lord. Amen.

FOR LITURGY PLANNERS

Liturgical Suggestions

Today is celebrated as 'Day for Life' in Ireland. Penitential Rite c-vii. Alternative opening prayer. Preface of Sundays in Ordinary Time 8. Eucharistic Prayer 3. Solemn Blessing 11 (Ordinary Time 2) contains a verse from the Second Reading.

Songs: 'Praise to the Holiest'; 'Eat This Bread'; 'Holy God We Praise Thy Name'.

The Week Ahead

Tuesday 4 October: St Francis of Assisi, patron of ecologists. Rosh Hashanah, Jewish New Year's Day. Ramadan begins today (Islam).
Wednesday 5 October: World Teachers' Day (UN).
Friday 7 October: Our Lady of the Rosary (First Friday).

TWENTY-EIGHTH SUNDAY IN ORDINARY TIME

FOR PRESIDERS

Opening Comment

Today is Emigrant Sunday, when all our exiles are remembered. We gather as fellow-pilgrims with them, all journeying to the great banquet of heaven. In our Communion today, we get a taste of what is to come.

Penitential Rite: As we prepare ourselves to share in this sacred meal, let us call to mind God's mercy (pause):
Lord Jesus, you raise us to new life: Lord, have mercy.
Lord Jesus, you forgive us our sins: Christ, have mercy.
Lord Jesus, you feed us with your body and blood: Lord, have mercy.

Introduction to the Scripture Readings

Isaiah 25:6-10 – A vision of the feast prepared for us in heaven, when death is no more and tears are a thing of the past.
Philippians 4:12-14, 19-20 – Paul thanks his flock in Philippi for their support, and speaks of his confidence in Christ.
Matthew 22:1-14 – A vision of the wedding banquet at the end of life.

The General Intercessions *(Samples)*

Introduction *(by the Presider)*
Brothers and sisters, let us make our prayers to God, who gently shepherds all the flock.

Intercessions *(announced by the deacon, cantor or another person)*

1.   For Christians,
     that their belief in life after death may sustain them in difficult times.
     (Pause for silent prayer)   Lord, hear us.

2.   For our emigrants, particularly those in any kind of need,
     that they may experience friendship and support. *(Pause for silent prayer)*   Lord, hear us.

3.   For those who come to our country as strangers,
     that they may receive the welcome all exiles appreciate. *(Pause for silent prayer)* Lord, hear us.

4.   For couples preparing for marriage,
     that the gentle shepherd may show them the right path to follow.
     (Pause for silent prayer)   Lord, hear us.

5.   For the dead, those who have died in foreign lands and all we have lost
     (especially N & N), that a place at the eternal banquet may be theirs.
     (Pause for silent prayer)   Lord, hear us.

6.   For those we love, particularly all who are in need of prayer at this time.
     (Long pause for silent prayer)   Lord, hear us.

Conclusion *(by the Presider)*
God our shepherd, you invite us to your table in heaven:
Give us the grace we need on our journey there, we pray, through Jesus Christ our Lord. Amen.

FOR LITURGY PLANNERS

Liturgical Suggestions

Penitential Rite c-vi. Or, if the full form of the Gospel is to be used, recall the baptism of all by blessing and sprinkling holy water. Alternative Opening Prayer. Shorter form of Gospel omits mention of baptismal garment, ie. Matthew 22:1-10. Preface of Sundays in Ordinary Time 6, or of the Holy Eucharist 2. Eucharistic Prayer 1. Solemn Blessing10 (Ordinary Time 1).

Songs: 'The Lord's my Shepherd'; 'Eat This Bread'; 'Stay with us Lord'.

The Week Ahead

Monday 10 October: World Mental Health Day (UN). Columbus Day (USA). Thanksgiving Day (Canada).
Thursday 13 October: Yom Kippur, the Jewish 'Day of Atonement'.
Saturday 15 October: St Teresa of Avila (patron of headache sufferers). World Rural Women's Day (UN).

TWENTY-NINTH SUNDAY IN ORDINARY TIME

FOR PRESIDERS

Opening Comment
As God's family in this place, we gather to worship. God is our king, we heed his Word and share the Bread of Life.

Penitential Rite: Preparing for this celebration, we remember our sinfulness, and recall how freely we are forgiven (pause)
I confess…

Introduction to the Scripture Readings
Isaiah 45:1, 4-6 – Cyrus the unbeliever is chosen by God to do a job, the job of being a good leader.
1 Thessalonians 1:1-5 – For four of the next five Sundays we read passages from Paul's letter to the Thessalonians. The letter opens today with Paul commending the people of Salonika for their faith.
Matthew 22:15-21 – The Pharisees try to trap Jesus with word games.

The General Intercessions *(Samples)*

Introduction *(by the Presider)*
Let us make known our intentions to our God of glory and power.

Intercessions *(announced by the deacon, cantor or another person)*

1. For those who lead the Church, the pope and all the bishops,
    that they may do so with faith and courage. *(Pause for silent prayer)*   Lord, hear us.

2. For leaders of nations, and all those elected to serve us,
    that they may fight corruption and injustice. *(Pause for silent prayer)*   Lord, hear us.

3. For tax collectors and all who work for the state,
    that they may respect the rights of all our citizens. *(Pause for silent prayer)*   Lord, hear us.

4. For those who collect money during our liturgies, and for all who contribute,
    that God may reward generous hearts. *(Pause for silent prayer)*   Lord, hear us.

5. For all who have gone before us in faith (especially N & N),
    that God may call them to his side in heaven. *(Pause for silent prayer)*   Lord, hear us.

6. For those who have asked our prayers, whom we remember now.
    (Long pause for silent prayer)   Lord, hear us.

Conclusion *(by the Presider)*
God of glory and power, you will judge the peoples in fairness:
Hear the prayers we make and graciously grant them, through Christ our Lord. Amen.

FOR LITURGY PLANNERS

Liturgical Suggestions
Affirm your church collectors during today's liturgy. Penitential Rite a (Confiteor). Alternative Opening Prayer. Preface of Sundays in Ordinary Time 5. Eucharistic Prayer 3. Solemn Blessing 14 (Sundays in Ordinary Time 5).

Songs: 'All People That On Earth Do Dwell'; 'All That I Am'; 'How Great Thou Art'.

The Week Ahead
Monday 17 October: World Day for the Eradication of Poverty (UN). Sukkot begins at sunset (Judaism).
Tuesday 18 October: St Luke the evangelist, patron of doctors and surgeons.
Saturday 22 October: Anniversary of the inauguration of the ministry of Pope John Paul II in 1978.

MISSION SUNDAY

FOR PRESIDERS

Opening Comment
'Witness to the Faith' is suggested as the theme for this year's Mission Sunday. We thank God for the faithful witness of missionaries and pray for the courage to imitate them where we live and work.

Penitential Rite: As we prepare ourselves for this celebration, let us call to mind God's generous mercy (pause):
Lord Jesus, you came to gather the nations into the peace of God's kingdom: Lord, have mercy.
You come in word and sacrament to strengthen us in holiness: Christ, have mercy.
You will come in glory with salvation for your people: Lord, have mercy.

Introduction to the Scripture Readings
Exodus 22:20-26 – The people of Israel are reminded that in bad times they depended on the kindness of strangers. They should therefore treat the weak and helpless with compassion.
1 Peter 3:15-18 – Peter writes that Christians should be able to give a reason for the hope that is in them.
Matthew 22:34-40 – Jesus discloses the greatest commandment: love of God and neighbour.

The General Intercessions *(Samples)*

Introduction *(by the Presider)*
God is our fortress and our strength, so let us bring forward our intentions:

Intercessions *(announced by the deacon, cantor or another person)*

1. That the lives of Christians may be marked by love of God and neighbour.
   (Pause for silent prayer)   Lord, hear us.

2. That, with renewed confidence, missionaries may bring the Good News to all nations.
   (Pause for silent prayer)   Lord, hear us.

3. That many may generously answer the call to be missionaries.
   (Pause for silent prayer)   Lord, hear us.

4. That the people in our midst from other countries
   may experience true Christian kindness. *(Pause for silent prayer)*   Lord, hear us.

5. That those who have died may follow the Lord into the Kingdom
   (especially N & N). *(Pause for silent prayer)*   Lord, hear us.

6. That we may have the divine assistance in all our needs,
   particularly those we remember now. *(Long pause for silent prayer)* Lord, hear us.

Conclusion *(by the Presider)*
O God of love, our rock, our fortress, our strength, we take refuge in you!
With confidence we present these prayers to you, through Christ our Lord. Amen.

FOR LITURGY PLANNERS

Liturgical Suggestions
Penitential Rite c-ii. First Reading and Gospel for the 30th Sunday in Ordinary Time (Year A). Second Reading of the 6th Sunday of Easter, Year A (Lectionary Volume I, page 535). Preface of Sundays in Ordinary Time 1. Eucharistic Prayer 2. Solemn Blessing 12 (Ordinary Time 3).

Songs: 'Be Thou My Vision'; 'Ag Críost an Síol'; 'Go Tell Everyone'.

The Week Ahead
Monday 24 October: United Nations Day (international).
Friday 28 October: Sts Simon & Jude (Jude is the patron of hopeless cases). Quds Day (Islam).
• *Clocks go back one hour next Saturday night/Sunday morning: Winter Time begins.*

THIRTY-FIRST SUNDAY IN ORDINARY TIME

FOR PRESIDERS

Opening Comment

God's message is still a living power among us, so we gather to listen and be challenged by it.

Penitential Rite: Confident of God's care and mercy, let us call to mind our sins: (pause)

You were sent to heal the contrite: Lord, have mercy.

You came to call sinners: Christ, have mercy.

You plead for us at the right hand of the Father: Lord, have mercy.

Introduction to the Scripture Readings

Malachi 1:14 to 2:2, 8-10 – A warning for priests and other religious leaders of God's anger with those who stray.

1 Thessalonians 2:7-9, 13 – Paul reminds the people of Salonika of his work in their midst, and commends their faith.

Matthew 23:1-12 – Jesus attacks the hypocrisy of the religious leaders of his time.

The General Intercessions (*Samples*)

Introduction (*by the Presider*)

Brothers and sisters, let us present our prayers to God, who takes pity on the humble.

Intercessions (*announced by the deacon, cantor or another person*)

1. For priests and bishops,
   that they may practise what they preach. (*Pause for silent prayer*)   Lord, hear us.

2. For those in leadership positions in church and state,
   that they may learn to be true servants. (*Pause for silent prayer*)   Lord, hear us.

3. For all who teach in schools and colleges,
   that they may share their knowledge with humility. (*Pause for silent prayer*)   Lord, hear us

4. For people who are sick, in mind or body,
   that God's healing power may bring them peace. (*Pause for silent prayer*)   Lord, hear us.

5. For those who have died (especially N & N),
   that their hope in God may be rewarded. (*Pause for silent prayer*)   Lord, hear us.

6. For all our own needs, which we remember in a moment of quiet prayer…
   (*Long pause for silent prayer*)   Lord, hear us

Conclusion (*by the Presider*)

God of all goodness, you grant the desires of the humble:

Hear the prayers we make and grant them, we pray, through Christ our Lord. Amen.

FOR LITURGY PLANNERS

Liturgical Suggestions

Penitential Rite c-i. Alternative Opening Prayer. Preface of Sundays in Ordinary Time 1. Eucharistic Prayer 3. Solemn Blessing 14 (Sundays in Ordinary Time 5).

Songs: 'Be Thou my Vision'; 'Will You Let me be Your Servant?', 'This is My Will'.

The Week Ahead

Monday 31 October: Hallowe'en — October Bank Holiday (Ireland).

Tuesday 1 November: All Saints Day (holyday of obligation).

Wednesday 2 November: All Souls Day (First day of November novena for the dead).

Thursday 3 November: Id al Fitr — End of Ramadan (Islam). National Culture Day (Japan).

ALL SAINTS DAY

FOR PRESIDERS

Opening Comment
Today and tomorrow we remember all the dead, those in heaven and those still on the way there: God alone knows where each soul is. Today's feast celebrates the saints in heaven, the holy men and women of every time and place: we hope some of our people are among them.

Penitential Rite: As we prepare ourselves to offer our praise with the saints, let us call to mind our sins: (pause)
Lord Jesus, you came to gather the nations into the peace of God's kingdom: Lord, have mercy.
You come in word and sacrament to strengthen us in holiness: Christ, have mercy.
You will come in glory with salvation for your people: Lord, have mercy.

Introduction to the Scripture Readings
Apocalypse 7:2-4, 9-14 – This was written to reassure Christians suffering during Nero's persecution. Christians today are marked as they were, through baptism, and promised God's protection.
1 John 3:1-3 – St John assures us of God's love and the hope for the future that comes with it.
Matthew 5:1-12 – The Gospel lists the kinds of people to whom the kingdom of heaven already belongs.

The General Intercessions *(Samples)*

Introduction *(by the Presider)*
Let us bring our prayers to God, who created the earth and its fullness.

Intercessions *(announced by the deacon, cantor or another person)*
1. For all the baptised,
    that they may enter the company of the saints. *(Pause for silent prayer)*   Lord, hear us.

2. For people of every nation, language and way of life,
    that they may work to rid this world of hatred and injustice.
    (Pause for silent prayer)   Lord, hear us.

3   For those whose lives are plagued by doubt and despair,
    that they may be supported by fellow pilgrims on the road to their eternal home.
    (Pause for silent prayer)   Lord, hear us.

4. For all the sick, particularly those who feel that death is near,
    that their friends who have already reached heaven may encourage them.
    (Pause for silent prayer)   Lord, hear us.

5. For all who have gone before us in faith (especially N & N),
    that they may stand with the saints before the throne of the Lamb.
    (Pause for silent prayer)   Lord, hear us.

6. For our own needs, for those who have asked our prayers, we pray quietly…
    (Long pause for silent prayer)   Lord, hear us.

Conclusion *(by the Presider)*
God of heaven and earth, you reward those with clean hands and pure hearts:
In our unworthiness we bring our prayers to you, through Christ our Lord.

FOR LITURGY PLANNERS

Liturgical Suggestions
Penitential Rite c-ii. Alternative Opening Prayer. Preface of All Saints. Eucharistic Prayer 3. Solemn Blessing 18 (All Saints). Use incense today, honouring the altar and cross, the Gospel book, gifts, *presider* and *people*.

Songs: 'Come to Me'; 'Faith of our Fathers'; 'Be Thou My Vision'; any song based on the Beatitudes.

ALL SOULS DAY

FOR PRESIDERS

Opening Comment

On All Saints Day and today, we remember all the dead, those in heaven and those still on the way there: God alone knows where each soul is. Today we pray for all souls, for the faithful departed still on the journey to their heavenly home.

Penitential Rite: As we prepare ourselves to renew our trust in God's mercy, let us call to mind our sins: (pause)
You raise the dead to life in the Spirit: Lord, have mercy.
You bring pardon and peace to the sinner: Christ, have mercy.
You bring light to those in darkness: Lord, have mercy.

Introduction to the Scripture Readings

Isaiah 25: 6-9 – A beautiful vision of the heavenly banquet that awaits believers, a sign of God's salvation.
Romans 5: 5-11 – Our hope comes from the death of Christ: through it, we can know how much we are loved by God.
Matthew 11:25-30 – To the weary, the Lord provides rest. We entrust our dead to his gentle care.

The General Intercessions *(Samples)*

Introduction *(by the Presider)*
Brothers and sisters, the Lord is our light and our help, so let us bring our prayers to God.

Intercessions *(announced by the deacon, cantor or another person)*
1. For all who follow Christ,
    that their faith in eternal life after death may be strong. *(Pause for silent prayer)* Lord, hear us.

2. For men and women who have been lost because of war or violence,
    that the tragedy of their deaths may spur humanity
    to build a world of peace and tolerance. *(Pause for silent prayer)* Lord, hear us.

3. For those who have died before their time, in accidents or through suicide,
    that their loss may remind all of the sacredness of human life,
    God's great gift to the world. *(Pause for silent prayer)* Lord, hear us

4. For people overcome by grief,
    that the power of Christ's love may lift them up and renew their hope.
    (Pause for silent prayer) Lord, hear us.

5. For all our relatives and friends who have gone before us in faith,
    whom we remember now; *(pause)*
    for the priests and people who worshipped here in times past; *(pause)*
    and for those who have died in the past year; *(pause)*
    that they may behold the Lord's temple in the new and eternal Jerusalem.
    (Pause for silent prayer) Lord, hear us.

Conclusion *(by the Presider)*
God of light, to live in your house is the desire of all your children:
Hear our prayers and help us in all our needs, through Christ our Lord.

FOR LITURGY PLANNERS

Liturgical Suggestions

Penitential Rite c-v. Mass prayers of Mass 1 for The Commemoration of All the Faithful Departed, page 654 (Roman Missal). Readings from Lectionary Volume 1, page 1002-1004 (Gospel year A). Preface of Christian Death 4. Eucharistic Prayer 2. Solemn Blessing 20 (The Dead). The names of the dead submitted by parishioners may be placed on a purple-covered table near the altar. A candle may be lit nearby and flowers placed: this 'shrine' remains in place for November Masses for the dead.

Songs: 'My Soul Is Longing For Your Peace'; 'Shepherd Me O God; 'Now The Green Blade Rises'.

THIRTY-SECOND SUNDAY IN ORDINARY TIME

FOR PRESIDERS

Opening Comment

At this time of year, our deceased relatives and friends are often in our minds. Our faith tells us that we needn't grieve over them like people with no hope. We remember them with love, and entrust them to God's care.

Penitential Rite: As we begin to celebrate God's enduring mercy, let us call to mind our moments of unfaithfulness: (pause)
Lord Jesus, you raise us to new life: Lord, have mercy.
Lord Jesus, you forgive us our sins: Christ, have mercy.
Lord Jesus, you feed us with your body and blood: Lord, have mercy.

Introduction to the Scripture Readings

Wisdom 6:12-16 – Wisdom is a gift freely given to those who seek it. Wisdom never disappoints.
1 Thessalonians 4:13-18 – We're assured that we needn't grieve over the dead like people with no hope.
Matthew 25: 1-13 – A warning against complacency: we need to be ready, to 'stay awake.'

The General Intercessions *(Samples)*

Introduction *(by the Presider)*
My sisters and brothers in Christ, God's love is better than life, so we present our prayers to the Lord:

Intercessions *(announced by the deacon, cantor or another person)*

1. For all who follow the Christian way,
    that they may receive the gift of wisdom. *(Pause for silent prayer)*   Lord, hear us.

2. For people looking forward to their marriage,
    that they may prepare wisely and well. *(Pause for silent prayer)*   Lord, hear us.

3. For all who grieve over the loss of a loved one,
    that they may be consoled by our loving support. *(Pause for silent prayer)*   Lord, hear us.

4. For those who support the grieving,
    that they themselves may be comforted when desolation comes their way.
    (Pause for silent prayer)   Lord, hear us

5. For all we have lost to death (especially N & N),
    that their hope in God may be rewarded. *(Pause for silent prayer)*   Lord, hear us.

6. For all our own particular needs, which we remember now.
    (Long pause for silent prayer)   Lord, hear us.

Conclusion *(by the Presider)*
O God of endless love, in the shadow of your wings we find refuge:
Hear the prayers we humbly make, through Jesus Christ our Lord. Amen.

FOR LITURGY PLANNERS

Liturgical Suggestions

Penitential rite c-vi. Or because the lamps of today's Gospel may be reflected in the candles lit at baptism, start with the blessing and sprinkling of holy water. First Opening Prayer. Preface of Sundays in Ordinary Time 4. Eucharistic Prayer 2. Solemn Blessing 2 (Sundays in Ordinary Time 11) or 20 (The Dead).

Songs: 'Sing a New Song Unto the Lord'; 'My Soul is Longing for your Peace'; 'Only in God'.

The Week Ahead

Monday 7 November: Day of Accord and Reconciliation in Russia (formerly the Socialist Revolution Anniversary)
Wednesday 9 November: The Opening of the Berlin Wall in 1989 is commemorated today.
Friday 11 November: St Martin of Tours, patron of France, soldiers, beggars and innkeepers. Today is Armistice Day, Remembrance Day and/or Veterans' Day in various countries.

THIRTY-THIRD SUNDAY IN ORDINARY TIME

FOR PRESIDERS

Opening Comment

The beginning of the Advent season is coming closer, and the Liturgy invites us to look further into the future, towards the end of time, to be ready when the Day of the Lord comes. Today's gathering will help us on our way, by teaching us how to live and giving us food for the journey.

Penitential Rite: To prepare ourselves for this celebration, let us call to mind God's faithfulness and our weakness: (pause)
Lord Jesus, you came to gather the nations into the peace of God's kingdom: Lord, have mercy.
You come in word and sacrament to strengthen us in holiness: Christ, have mercy.
You will come in glory with salvation for your people: Lord, have mercy.

Introduction to the Scripture Readings

Proverbs 31:10-13, 19-20, 30-31 – The different talents people possess are highlighted in today's readings. The first describes some of the gifts a woman can bring to marriage.

1 Thessalonians 5:1-6 – We're reminded that the Day of the Lord could come at any moment, so we must be on the watch.

Matthew 25:14-30 – The talents we receive are given to us for a purpose – to be used.

The General Intercessions *(Samples)*

> **Introduction** *(by the Presider)*
> Brothers and sisters, let us make our prayers known to the Lord, who blesses those who learn to trust:
>
> **Intercessions** *(announced by the deacon, cantor or another person)*

1.   For all the members of the Christian community,
      that we may use our talents well, putting them at the service of all.
      (Pause for silent prayer)   Lord, hear us.

2.   For an increase in the number of those who volunteer their services,
      that charities and other organisations may not lack good help.
      (Pause for silent prayer)   Lord, hear us.

3.   For wives and husbands,
      that they may value each other's gifts, and be generous to the needy.
      (Pause for silent prayer)   Lord, hear us

4.   For prisoners, and their families, that they may put their trust in God,
      who never forgets them. *(Pause for silent prayer)*   Lord, hear us.

5.   For people who are sick, in mind, body or spirit,
      that our prayers and practical concern may support them. *(Pause for silent prayer)* Lord, hear us.

6.   For those who have died as the result of war or violence, at home or abroad,
      whom we remember in silence *(pause)*; that all who have been lost to death
      may receive the crown of life. *(Pause for silent prayer)*   Lord, hear us.

> **Conclusion** *(by the Presider)*
> Eternal God, you bless those who trust in you: hear the prayers we make, through Christ our Lord. Amen.

FOR LITURGY PLANNERS

Liturgical Suggestions

Restorative Justice Week begins today (formerly Prisoner's Week). Prayers on that theme may be used at weekday Masses: see Roman Missal page 837 and Lectionary Volume III pages 677-685, also page 667. Penitential Rite c-ii. Preface of Sundays in Ordinary Time 7. Eucharistic Prayer 1. Solemn Blessing 1 (Ordinary Time 10).

Songs: 'Lord of all Hopefulness'; 'All that I Am'; 'Shepherd Me O God'.

The Week Ahead

Tuesday 15 November: St Albert the Great, patron of scientists. King's Birthday (Belgium).
Wednesday 16 November: International Day for Tolerance (UN).
Saturday 19 November: National Commemoration Day, Monaco.

CHRIST THE KING

FOR PRESIDERS

Opening Comment
Today we celebrate the feast of Christ the King. At the end of time, this King will come in glory to judge the living and the dead. He will ask how we treated the hungry and thirsty, the stranger, the naked, those sick or in prison.
> *Penitential Rite: As we prepare ourselves to honour our king, let us call to mind the times we failed in love: (pause)* I confess...

Introduction to the Scripture Readings
Ezekiel 34:11-12, 15-17 – Our King is like a shepherd who minds all the sheep, particularly those in special need.
1 Corinthians 15:20-26, 28 – As King, Christ has conquered all, even death itself.
Matthew 25:31-36 – Our King will reward those who look after people in need.

The General Intercessions *(Samples)*

Introduction *(by the Presider)*
Let us present our prayers to God, the shepherd who cares for all the flock:

Intercessions *(announced by the deacon, cantor or another person)*

1. For those in leadership roles in the Church, that they may show the kindness and sensitivity of the Good Shepherd. *(Pause for silent prayer)* — Lord, hear us.

2. For leaders of governments and nations, that they may work for justice and truth. *(Pause for silent prayer)* — Lord, hear us.

3. For those who visit us as strangers that we may give a warm welcome to refugees and immigrants. *(Pause for silent prayer)* — Lord, hear us.

4. For our brothers and sisters in prison, that we may not forget our duty to care for them and their families. *(Pause for silent prayer)* — Lord, hear us.

5. For those who have passed beyond this world (especially N & N), that they may dwell in the Lord's house for ever. *(Pause for silent prayer)* — Lord, hear us.

6. For the people we love – particularly those in need of support at this time, whom we remember quietly. *(Long pause for silent prayer)* — Lord, hear us.

Conclusion *(by the Presider)*
Loving God, caring shepherd, you look after your people at every moment of their lives:
Hear the prayers we make, in trust and faith, through Christ our Lord. Amen

FOR LITURGY PLANNERS

Liturgical Suggestions
Sing a popular hymn of praise at every celebration this weekend to honour the feast. Use incense at the start of Mass, for the Gospel and the Gifts. Penitential Rite a (Confiteor). Alternative Opening Prayer. Preface of Christ the King (no. 51). Eucharistic Prayer 3. Solemn Blessing 13 (Ordinary Time 4).

Songs: 'Hail Redeemer'; 'Holy God We Praise Thy Name'; 'Praise My Soul The King of Heaven'; 'O Praise Ye The Lord' etc.

The Week Ahead
Wednesday 23 November: St Columbanus (or Columban), missionary.
Thursday 24 November: Thanksgiving Day (USA).
Friday 25 November: International Day for the Elimination of Violence Against Women (UN).
• *Next Sunday is the First Sunday of Advent (Year B).*

SUNDAYS AND FEASTDAYS OF DECEMBER 2005

First Sunday of Advent (27 November 2005)
Readings: Isaiah 63: 16-17, 64:1, 3-8 • I Corinthians 1:3-9 • Mark 13:33-37
For general themes for use in composing the Prayer of the Faithful and other liturgy ideas, please see page 7.

Second Sunday of Advent (4 December 2005)
Readings: Isaiah 40:1-5, 9-11 • 2 Peter 3:8-14 • Mark 1:1-8
For general themes for use in composing the Prayer of the Faithful and other liturgy ideas, please see page 8.

Immaculate Conception of the BVM (Thursday, 8 December 2005)
For ideas for presiders and liturgy planners, please see page 9.

Third Sunday of Advent (11 December 2005)
Readings: Isaiah 61:1-2, 10-11 • 1 Thessalonians 5:16-24 • John 1:6-8, 19-28
For general themes for use in composing the Prayer of the Faithful and other liturgy ideas, please see page 12.

Fourth Sunday of Advent (18 December 2005)
Readings: Samuel 7:1-5, 8-12, 14, 16 • Romans 16:25-27 • Luke 1:26-38
For general themes for use in composing the Prayer of the Faithful and other liturgy ideas, please see page 13.

Nativity of the Lord/Christmas (Saturday-Sunday, 24-25 December 2005)
For ideas for presiders and liturgy planners for the four Christmas Masses, please see pages 14-17.

Solemnity of Mary, Mother of God/New Year's Day (Sunday, 1 January 2006)
For ideas for presiders and liturgy planners, please see page 19.

FORWARD PLANNING FOR THE LITURGY
2006-2015

Year	Ash Wednesday	Easter Sunday	Pentecost	Corpus Christi (after which the Sundays of Ordinary Time restart)	Christ the King (by which time material for the new liturgical year should be acquired)
2006 (Year B)	1 March	16 April	4 June	18 June	26 November
2007 (Year C)	21 February	8 April	27 May	10 June	25 November
2008 (Year A)	**6 February**	**23 March**	**11 May**	**25 May**	**23 November**
2009 (Year B)	25 February	12 April	31 May	14 June	22 November
2010 (Year C)	17 February	4 April	23 May	6 June	21 November
2011 (Year A)	**9 March**	**24 April**	**12 June**	**26 June**	**20 November**
2012 (Year B)	22 February	8 April	27 May	10 June	25 November
2013 (Year C)	13 February	31 March	19 May	2 June	24 November
2014 (Year A)	**5 March**	**20 April**	**8 June**	**22 June**	**23 November**
2015 (Year B)	18 February	5 April	24 May	7 June	22 November